# CAMBRIDGE LIBRARY COLLECTION

*Books of enduring scholarly value*

## English Men of Letters

In the 1870s, Macmillan publishers began to issue a series of books called 'English Men of Letters' – biographies of English writers by other English writers. The general editor of the series was the journalist, critic, politician, and supporter (and later biographer) of Gladstone, John Morley (1838–1923). The aim was to provide a short introduction to each subject and his works, but also that the life should illuminate the works, and vice versa. The subjects range chronologically from Chaucer to Thackeray and Dickens, and an important feature of the series is that many of the authors (Henry James on Hawthorne, Ward on Dickens) were discussing writers of the previous generation, and some (Trollope on Thackeray) had even known their subjects personally. The series exemplifies the British approach to literary biography and criticism at the end of the nineteenth century, and also reveals which authors were at that time regarded as canonical.

## Byron

George Gordon, Lord Byron (1788–1824) is regarded as one of Britain's greatest poets. As famous for his personality as he was for his poetry, he was rebellious, extravagant and controversial, his life peppered with scandal. First published in the English Men of Letters series in 1880, this biography by John Nichol (1833–94), who also wrote on Carlyle for the series, argues that while Byron did not shape the Romantic era, his work was still highly influential on his contemporaries. Setting Byron's work in an historical context, Nichol shows how the society of his time both idolised him and condemned him as a moral outcast; he was also greatly admired for his efforts for the liberation of Greece from the Ottoman Empire, during which he died. Nichol also discusses the creation of the 'Byronic hero', as much a reflection of Byron's flamboyant persona as an invented literary character.

Cambridge University Press has long been a pioneer in the reissuing of out-of-print titles from its own backlist, producing digital reprints of books that are still sought after by scholars and students but could not be reprinted economically using traditional technology. The Cambridge Library Collection extends this activity to a wider range of books which are still of importance to researchers and professionals, either for the source material they contain, or as landmarks in the history of their academic discipline.

Drawing from the world-renowned collections in the Cambridge University Library, and guided by the advice of experts in each subject area, Cambridge University Press is using state-of-the-art scanning machines in its own Printing House to capture the content of each book selected for inclusion. The files are processed to give a consistently clear, crisp image, and the books finished to the high quality standard for which the Press is recognised around the world. The latest print-on-demand technology ensures that the books will remain available indefinitely, and that orders for single or multiple copies can quickly be supplied.

The Cambridge Library Collection will bring back to life books of enduring scholarly value (including out-of-copyright works originally issued by other publishers) across a wide range of disciplines in the humanities and social sciences and in science and technology.

# Byron

John Nichol

CAMBRIDGE UNIVERSITY PRESS

Cambridge, New York, Melbourne, Madrid, Cape Town,
Singapore, São Paolo, Delhi, Tokyo, Mexico City

Published in the United States of America by Cambridge University Press, New York

www.cambridge.org
Information on this title: www.cambridge.org/9781108034555

© in this compilation Cambridge University Press 2011

This edition first published 1880
This digitally printed version 2011

ISBN 978-1-108-03455-5 Paperback

This book reproduces the text of the original edition. The content and language reflect
the beliefs, practices and terminology of their time, and have not been updated.

Cambridge University Press wishes to make clear that the book, unless originally published
by Cambridge, is not being republished by, in association or collaboration with, or
with the endorsement or approval of, the original publisher or its successors in title.

# English Men of Letters

EDITED BY JOHN MORLEY

# BYRON

# BYRON

BY

JOHN NICHOL

London:
MACMILLAN AND CO.
1880.

FOURTH THOUSAND.

# CONTENTS.

# BOOKS CONSULTED.

# GENEALOGY OF THE BYRON FAMILY.

# THE BYRON FAMILY, FROM THE CONQUEST.

Ralph de Burun (estates in Nottingham and Derby).

Hugh de Burun (Lord of Horestan).

Hugh de Buron (became a monk),

Sir Roger de Buron (gave lands to monks of Swinstead).

Cecilia = Robert de Byron.

Robert de Byron.

Sir John Byron (Governor of York under Edward I.).

Sir Richard Clayton.

Sir John (knighted at siege of Calais).

Sir Richard Byron.

Sir John (knighted in 3rd year of Henry V.).

Sir John Butler. = Sir Nicholas.

Alice

Sir Nicholas (made K.B. at marriage of Prince Arthur; died 1503).

Sir John (knighted by Richmond at Milford; fought at Bosworth; died 1468).

2nd wife, widow of George Haigh = Sir John Byron (received grant of Newstead from Henry VIII., May 26, 154).

Bar Sinister.

Sir Nicholas Strelleye.

Alice = John Byron, of Clayton (inherited by gift, knighted by Elizabeth, 1579).

Sir Richard Molyneux.

Anne = Sir John (K.B. at coronation of James I.; Governor of Tower).

Sir Nicholas (at Edgehill; Governor of Chester; prisoner to the Parliament).

(Buried at Hucknall Torkard) RICHARD, 2nd Lord (1605—1679).

Sir JOHN, 1st Lord (created Baron Byron, of Rochdale, Oct. 24, 1643; at Newbury, Edgehill, Chester, &c.; Governor of Duke of York; died at Paris, 1662).

Viscount Chaworth.

Elizabeth = WILLIAM, 3rd Lord (died 1695).

Lord Berkeley.

WILLIAM, 4th Lord (1669—1736) = Frances (3rd wife).

Isabella = Lord Carlisle.

Admiral John (1723—1786; "Foul-weather Jack").

Lord Carlisle (the poet's guardian).

WILLIAM, 5th Lord (1722—1798) [killed Mr. Chaworth; survived his sons and a grandson, who died 1794; called "The wicked Lord"].

A daughter. Colonel Leigh.

George Anson (1758—1793).

1. Marchioness of Carmarthen } = John Byron (1751—1791) = 2. Miss Gordon, of Gight.

GEORGE GORDON, 6th Lord (1788—1824). Married Anna Isabella (1792—1860), daughter of Sir Ralph Milbanke and Judith, daughter of Sir Edward Noel (Viscount Wentworth), and by her had

Admiral GEORGE ANSON, 7th Lord (1789—1868).

(1783—1851) Augusta = Colonel Leigh. Several daughters.

Earl Lovelace = Augusta-Ada (1815—1852).

Frederick.

GEORGE, 8th Lord (1818—1870).

Ralph Gordon, now Lord Wentworth.

Byron Noel (died 1862).

GEORGE F. WILLIAM, 9th and present Lord Byron.

Mr. Blunt = Lady Anne.

# BYRON.

## CHAPTER I.

### ANCESTRY AND FAMILY.

BYRON'S life was passed under the fierce light that beats upon an intellectual throne. He succeeded in making himself—what he wished to be—the most notorious personality in the world of letters of our century. Almost every one who came in contact with him has left on record various impressions of intimacy or interview. Those whom he excluded or patronized, maligned; those to whom he was genial, loved him. Mr. Southey, in all sincerity, regarded him as the principle of Evil incarnate; an American writer of tracts in the form of stories is of the same opinion: to the Countess Guiccioli he is an archangel. Mr. Carlyle considers him to have been a mere "sulky dandy." Goethe ranks him as the first English poet after Shakespeare, and is followed by the leading critics of France, Italy, and Spain. All concur in the admission that Byron was as proud of his race as of his verse, and that in unexampled measure the good and evil of his nature were inherited and inborn. His genealogy is, therefore, a matter of no idle antiquarianism.

B

There are legends of old Norse Buruns migrating from
their home in Scandinavia, and settling, one branch in
Normandy, another in Livonia.   To the latter belonged
a shadowy Marshal de Burun, famous for the almost
absolute power he wielded in the then infant realm of
Russia.   Two members of the family came over with the
Conqueror, and settled in England.   Of Erneis de Burun,
who had lands in York and Lincoln, we hear little more.
Ralph, the poet's ancestor, is mentioned in Doomsday
Book—our first authentic record—as having estates in
Nottinghamshire and Derby.   His son Hugh was lord of
Horestan Castle in the latter county, and with his son
of the same name, under King Stephen, presented the
church of Ossington to the monks of Lenton.   The
latter Hugh joined their order; but the race was continued by his son Sir Roger, who gave lands to the
monastery of Swinstead.   This brings us to the reign
of Henry II. (1155—1189), when Robert de Byron
adopted the spelling of his name afterwards retained, and
by his marriage with Cecilia, heir of Sir Richard Clayton,
added to the family possessions an estate in Lancashire,
where, till the time of Henry VIII., they fixed their
seat.   The poet, relying on old wood-carvings at Newstead, claims for some of his ancestors a part in the
crusades, and mentions a name not apparently belonging
to that age—

Near Ascalon's towers, John of Horestan slumbers—

a romance, like many of his, possibly founded on fact, but
incapable of verification.

Two grandsons of Sir Robert have a more substantial
fame, having served with distinction in the wars of

Edward I. The elder of these was governor of the city
of York. Some members of his family fought at Cressy,
and one of his sons, Sir John, was knighted by Edward
III. at the siege of Calais. Descending through the
other, Sir Richard, we come to another Sir John,
knighted by Richmond, afterwards Henry VII., on his
landing at Milford. He fought, with his kin, on the field
of Bosworth, and dying without issue, left the estates to his
brother, Sir Nicholas, knighted in 1502, at the marriage
of Prince Arthur. The son of Sir Nicholas, known as
"little Sir John of the great beard," appears to have
been a favourite of Henry VIII., who made him Steward
of Manchester and Lieutenant of Sherwood, and on the
dissolution of the monasteries presented him with the
Priory of Newstead, the rents of which were equivalent
to about 4000*l.* of our money. Sir John, who stepped
into the Abbey in 1540, married twice, and the premature
appearance of a son by the second wife—widow of Sir
George Halgh—brought the bar sinister of which so much
has been made. No indication of this fact, however,
appears in the family arms, and it is doubtful if the poet
was aware of a reproach which in any case does not touch
his descent. The "filius naturalis," John Byron of
Clayton, inherited by deed of gift, and was knighted by
Queen Elizabeth in 1579. His descendants were prominent as staunch Royalists during the whole period of the
Civil Wars. At Edgehill there were seven Byrons on
the field.

> On Marston, with Rupert 'gainst traitors contending,
> Four brothers enrich'd with their blood the bleak field.

Sir Nicholas, one of the seven, is extolled as " a person of
great affability and dexterity, as well as martial knowledge,

which gave great life to the designs of the well affected."
He was taken prisoner by the Parliament while acting as
governor of Chester. Under his nephew, Sir John,
Newstead is said to have been besieged and taken; but
the knight escaped, in the words of the poet—never a
Radical at heart—a " protecting genius,

> For nobler combats here reserved his life,
> To lead the band where godlike Falkland fell."

Clarendon, indeed, informs us, that on the morning before
the battle, Falkland, " very cheerful, as always upon
action, put himself into the first rank of the Lord Byron's
regiment." This slightly antedates his title. The first
battle of Newbury was fought on September, 1643. For
his services there, and at a previous royal victory, over
Waller in July, Sir John was, on October 24th of the same
year, created Baron of Rochdale, and so became the first
Peer of the family.

This first lord was succeeded by his brother Richard
(1605—1679), famous in the war for his government and
gallant defence of Newark. He rests in the vault that
now contains the dust of the greatest of his race, in Hucknall Torkard Church, where his epitaph records the fact
that the family lost all their present fortunes by their
loyalty, adding, " yet it pleased God so to bless the
humble endeavours of the said Richard, Lord Byron, that
he repurchased part of their ancient inheritance, which
he left to his posterity, with a laudable memory for his
great piety and charity." His eldest son, William, the
third Lord (died 1695), is worth remembering on
two accounts. He married Elizabeth, the daughter of
Viscount Chaworth, and so wove the first link in a
strange association of tragedy and romance : he was a

patron of one of those poets who, approved by neither
gods nor columns, are remembered by the accident of
an accident, and was himself a poetaster, capable of the
couplet, —

> My whole ambition only does extend
> To gain the name of Shipman's faithful friend, —

an ambition which, considering its moderate scope, may
be granted to have attained its desire.

His successor, the fourth lord (1669—1736), gentleman
of the bedchamber to Prince George of Denmark, himself
living a quiet life, became, by his third wife, Frances,
daughter of Lord Berkeley, the progenitor of a strange
group of eccentric, adventurous, and passionate spirits.
The eldest son, the fifth lord, and immediate predecessor
in the peerage of the poet, was born in 1722, entered the
naval service, left his ship, the " Victory," just before she
was lost on the rocks of Alderney, and subsequently
became master of the stag-hounds. In 1765, the year of
the passing of the American Stamp Act, an event occurred
which coloured the whole of his after-life, and is curiously
illustrative of the manners of the time. On January 26th
or 29th (accounts vary) ten members of an aristocratic
social club sat down to dinner in Pall-mall. Lord Byron
and Mr. Chaworth, his neighbour and kinsman, were of
the party. In the course of the evening, when the wine
was going round, a dispute arose between them about
the management of game, so frivolous that one conjectures the quarrel to have been picked to cloak some
other cause of offence. Bets were offered, and high
words passed, but the company thought the matter had
blown over. On going out, however, the disputants
met on the stairs, and one of the two, it is uncertain

which, cried out to the waiter to show them an empty
room. This was done, and a single tallow candle being
placed on the table, the door was shut. A few minutes
later a bell was rung, and the hotel master rushing in,
Mr. Chaworth was found mortally wounded. There had
been a struggle in the dim light, and Byron, having
received the first lunge harmlessly in his waistcoat, had
shortened his sword and run his adversary through the
body, with the boast, not uncharacteristic of his grand
nephew, " By G—d, I have as much courage as any man
in England." A coroner's inquest was held, and he was
committed to the Tower on a charge of murder. The
interest in the trial which subsequently took place in
Westminster Hall, was so great that tickets of admission
were sold for six guineas. The peers, after two days' discussion, unanimously returned a verdict of manslaughter.
Byron, pleading his privileges, and paying his fees, was
set at liberty ; but he appears henceforth as a spectre-
haunted man, roaming about under false names, or shut
up in the Abbey like a baited savage, shunned by his
fellows high and low, and the centre of the wildest
stories. That he shot a coachman, and flung the body
into the carriage beside his wife, who very sensibly
left him ; that he tried to drown her ; that he had
devils to attend him—were among the many weird
legends of " the wicked lord." The poet himself says that
his ancestor's only companions were the crickets that
used to crawl over him, receive stripes with straws
when they misbehaved, and on his death made an
exodus in procession from the house. When at home
he spent his time in pistol-shooting, making sham
fights with wooden ships about the rockeries of the
lake, and building ugly turrets on the battlements.

He hated his heir presumptive, sold the estate of
Rochdale,—a proceeding afterwards challenged—and cut
down the trees of Newstead, to spite him ; but he survived his three sons, his brother, and his only grandson, who was killed in Corsica in 1794.

On his own death in 1798, the estates and title
passed to George Gordon, then a child of ten, whom
he used to talk of, without a shadow of interest, as
" the little boy who lives at Aberdeen." His sister
Isabella married Lord Carlisle, and became the mother
of the fifth Earl, the poet's nominal guardian. She
was a lady distinguished for eccentricity of manners,
and (like her son satirized in the *Bards and Reviewers*)
for the perpetration of indifferent verses. The career of
the fourth lord's second son, John, the poet's grand-
father, recalls that of the sea-kings from whom the
family claim to have sprung. Born in 1723, he at an
early age entered the naval service, and till his death in
1786 was tossed from storm to storm. " He had no rest
on sea, nor I on shore," writes his illustrious descendant.
In 1740 a fleet of five ships was sent out under
Commodore Anson to annoy the Spaniards, with whom
we were then at war, in the South Seas. Byron took
service as a midshipman in one of those ships—all
more or less unfortunate—called " The Wager." Being
a bad sailor, and heavily laden, she was blown from her
company, and wrecked in the Straits of Magellan. The
majority of the crew were cast on a bleak rock, which
they christened Mount Misery. After encountering all
the horrors of mutiny and famine, and being in various
ways deserted, five of the survivors, among them Captain
Cheap and Mr. Byron, were taken by some Patagonians
to the Island of Chiloe, and thence, after some months,

to Valparaiso. They were kept for nearly two years
as prisoners at St. Iago, the capital of Chili, and in
December, 1744, put on board a French frigate, which
reached Brest in October, 1745. Early in 1746 they
arrived at Dover in a Dutch vessel.

This voyage is the subject of a well-known apostrophe
in *The Pleasures of Hope*, beginning—

> And such thy strength-inspiring aid that bore
> The hardy Byron from his native shore.
> In torrid climes, where Chiloe's tempests sweep
> Tumultuous murmurs o'er the troubled deep,
> 'Twas his to mourn misfortune's rudest shock,
> Scourged by the winds and cradled by the rock.

Byron's own account of his adventures, published in 1768,
is remarkable for freshness of scenery like that of our first
literary traveller, Sir John Mandeville, and a force of description which recalls Defoe. It interests us more especially from the use that has been made of it in that
marvellous mosaic of voyages, the shipwreck, in *Don
Juan*, the hardships of his hero being, according to the
poet—

> Comparative
> To those related in my grand-dad's narrative.

In June, 1764, Byron sailed with two ships, the
"Dolphin" and the "Tamar," on a voyage of discovery arranged by Lord Egmont, to seek a southern continent, in
the course of which he took possession of the largest of the
Falkland Islands, again passed through the Magellanic
Straits, and sailing home by the Pacific, circumnavigated
the globe. The planets so conspired that, though his
affable manners and considerate treatment made him always

popular with his men, sailors became afraid to serve under
" foul-weather Jack." In 1748 he married the daughter
of a Cornish squire, John Trevanion. They had two sons
and three daughters. One of the latter married her
cousin (the fifth lord's eldest son), who died in 1776,
leaving as his sole heir the youth who fell in the Mediterranean in 1794.

The eldest son of the veteran, John Byron, father of
the poet, was born in 1751, educated at Westminster, and,
having received a commission, became a captain in the
guards ; but his character, fundamentally unprincipled,
soon developed itself in such a manner as to alienate
him from his family. In 1778, under circumstances of
peculiar effrontery, he seduced Amelia D'Arcy, the
daughter of the Earl of Holdernesse, in her own right
Countess Conyers, then wife of the Marquis of Carmarthen, afterwards Duke of Leeds. " Mad Jack," as he
was called, seems to have boasted of his conquest ; but
the marquis, to whom his wife had hitherto been devoted,
refused to believe the rumours that were afloat, till an
intercepted letter, containing a remittance of money, for
which Byron, in reverse of the usual relations, was always
clamouring, brought matters to a crisis. The pair de-
camped to the continent ; and in 1779, after the marquis
had obtained a divorce, they were regularly married.
Byron seems to have been not only profligate but heartless, and he made life wretched to the woman he was even
more than most husbands bound to cherish. She died
in 1784, having given birth to two daughters. One died
in infancy ; the other was Augusta, the half sister and
good genius of the poet, whose memory remains like a
star on the fringe of a thunder-cloud, only brighter by
the passing of the smoke of calumny. In 1807 she

married Colonel Leigh, and had a numerous family, most
of whom died young. Her eldest daughter, Georgiana,
married Mr. Henry Trevanion. The fourth, Medora, had
an unfortunate history, the nucleus of an impertinent
and happily ephemeral romance.

The year after the death of his first wife, John Byron,
who seems to have had the fascinations of a Barry
Lyndon, succeeded in entrapping a second. This was
Miss Catherine Gordon of Gight, a lady with considerable estates in Aberdeenshire—which attracted the ad-
venturer—and an overweening Highland pride in her
descent from James I., the greatest of the Stuarts,
through his daughter Annabella, and the second Earl of
Huntly. This union suggested the ballad of an old
rhymer, beginning—

O whare are ye gaen, bonny Miss Gordon,
O whare are ye gaen, sae bonny and braw ?
Ye've married, ye've married wi' Johnny Byron,
To squander the lands o' Gight awa'.

The prophecy was soon fulfilled. The property of the
Scotch heiress was squandered with impetuous rapidity
by the English rake. In 1786 she left Scotland for
France, and returned to England toward the close of the
following year. On the 22nd of January, 1788, in
Holles Street, London, Mrs. Byron gave birth to her
only child, George Gordon, sixth Lord. Shortly after,
being pressed by his creditors, the father abandoned
both, and leaving them with a pittance of 150*l.* a year,
fled to Valenciennes, where he died, in August, 1791.

## CHAPTER II.

SOON after the birth of her son, Mrs. Byron took him to
Scotland. After spending some time with a relation,
she, early in 1790, settled in a small house at Aberdeen.
Ere long her husband, who had in the interval dissipated
away his remaining means, rejoined her; and they lived
together in humble lodgings, until their tempers, alike
fiery and irritable, compelled a definite separation. They
occupied apartments, for some time, at the opposite ends
of the same street, and interchanged visits. Being accustomed to meet the boy and his nurse, the father expressed a wish that the former should be sent to live
with him, at least for some days. "To this request,"
Moore informs us, "Mrs. Byron was at first not very
willing to accede; but, on the representation of the nurse
that if he kept him over one night he would not do
so another, she consented. On inquiring next morning
after the child, she was told by Captain Byron that he
had had quite enough of his young visitor." After a short
stay in the north, the Captain, extorting enough money
from his wife to enable him to fly from his creditors,
escaped to France. His absence must have been a relief; but his death is said to have so affected the
unhappy lady, that her shrieks disturbed the neighbour-

hood. The circumstance recalls an anecdote of a similar
outburst—attested by Sir W. Scott, who was present
on the occasion—before her marriage. Being present
at a representation, in Edinburgh, of the *Fatal Marriage*, when Mrs. Siddons was personating Isabella, Miss
Gordon was seized with a fit, and carried out of the
theatre, screaming out "O my Biron, my Biron." All
we know of her character shows it to have been not
only proud, impulsive, and wayward, but hysterical. She
constantly boasted of her descent, and clung to the courtesy title of "honourable," to which she had no claim.
Her affection and anger were alike demonstrative, her
temper never for an hour secure. She half worshipped,
half hated, the blackguard to whom she was married, and
took no steps to protect her property ; her son she alternately petted and abused. "Your mother's a fool !" said
a school companion to him years after. "I know it," was
his unique and tragic reply. Never was poet born to so
much illustrious, and to so much bad blood. The records
of his infancy betray the temper which he preserved
through life—passionate, sullen, defiant of authority, but
singularly amenable to kindness. On being scolded by
his first nurse for having soiled a dress, without utter-
ing a word he tore it from top to seam, as he had
seen his mother tear her caps and gowns ; but her sister
and successor in office, May Gray, acquired and retained
a hold over his affections, to which he has borne grateful
testimony. To her training is attributed the early and
remarkable knowledge of the Scriptures, especially of the
Psalms, which he possessed : he was, according to her
later testimony, peculiarly inquisitive and puzzling about
religion. Of the sense of solitude, induced by his earliest
impressions, he characteristically makes a boast. "My

daughter, my wife, my half-sister, my mother, my sister's mother, my natural daughter, and myself, are or were all only children. But the fiercest animals have the fewest numbers in their litters, as lions, tigers, &c."

To this practical orphanhood, and inheritance of feverish passion, there was added another, and to him a heavy and life-long burden. A physical defect in a healthy nature may either pass without notice or be turned to a high purpose. No line of his work reveals the fact that Sir Walter Scott was lame. The infirmity failed to cast even a passing shade over that serene power. Milton's blindness is the occasion of the noblest prose and verse of resignation in the language. But to understand Pope, we must remember that he was a cripple : and Byron never allows us to forget, because he himself never forgot it. Accounts differ as to the extent and origin of his deformity ; and the doubts on the matter are not removed by the inconsistent accounts of the indelicate post-mortem examination made by Mr. Trelawny at Mesolonghi. It is certain that one of the poet's feet was, either at birth or at a very early period, so seriously clubbed or twisted as to affect his gait, and to a considerable extent his habits. It also appears that the surgical means—boots, bandages, &c.—adopted to straighten the limb, only aggravated the evil. His sensitiveness on the subject was early awakened by careless or unfeeling references. " What a pretty boy Byron is," said a friend of his nurse. " What a pity he has such a leg." On which the child, with flashing eyes, cutting at her with a baby's whip, cried out, " Dinna speak of it." His mother herself, in her violent fits, when the boy ran round the room laughing at her attempts to catch him, used to say he was a little dog, as bad as his father, and to call him " a lame

brat "—an incident, which, notoriously suggested the
opening scene of the *Deformed Transformed.* In the
height of his popularity he fancied that the beggars
and street-sweepers in London were mocking him. He
satirized and discouraged dancing; he preferred riding
and swimming to other exercises, because they concealed his weakness; and on his death-bed asked to be
blistered in such a way that he might not be called on to
expose it. The Countess Guiccioli, Lady Blessington,
and others, assure us that in society few would have
observed the defect if he had not referred to it; but it
was never far from the mind, and therefore never far from
the mouth, of the least reticent of men.

In 1792 he was sent to a rudimentary day school of
girls and boys, taught by a Mr. Bowers, where he seems
to have learnt nothing save to repeat monosyllables by
rote. He next passed through the hands of a devout and
clever clergyman, named Ross, under whom according to
his own account he made astonishing progress, being
initiated into the study of Roman history, and taking
special delight in the battle of Regillus. Long afterwards,
when standing on the heights of Tusculum and looking
down on the little round lake, he remembered his young
enthusiasm and his old instructor. He next came under
the charge of a tutor called Paterson, whom he describes
as "a very serious, saturnine, but kind young man. He
was the son of my shoemaker, but a good scholar. With
him I began Latin, and continued till I went to the
grammar school, where I threaded all the classes to the
fourth, when I was recalled to England by the demise of
my uncle."

Of Byron's early school days there is little further record.
We learn from scattered hints that he was backward in

technical scholarship, and low in his class, in which he
seems to have had no ambition to stand high; but that
he eagerly took to history and romance, especially
luxuriating in the *Arabian Nights*. He was an indifferent penman, and always disliked mathematics ; but was
noted by masters and mates as of quick temper, eager for
adventures, prone to sports, always more ready to give a
blow than to take one, affectionate, though resentful.

When his cousin was killed at Corsica, in 1794, he
became the next heir to the title. In 1797, a friend,
meaning to compliment the boy, said, " We shall have the
pleasure some day of reading your speeches in the House
of Commons," he, with precocious consciousness, replied,
" I hope not. If you read any speeches of mine, it will
be in the House of Lords." Similarly, when, in the course
of the following year, the fierce old man at Newstead died,
and the young lord's name was called at school with
" Dominus " prefixed to it, his emotion was so great that
he was unable to answer, and burst into tears.

Belonging to this period is the somewhat shadowy
record of a childish passion for a distant cousin slightly
his senior, Mary Duff, with whom he claims to have
fallen in love in his ninth year. We have a quaint
picture of the pair sitting on the grass together, the girl's
younger sister beside them playing with a doll. A
German critic gravely remarks, " This strange phenomenon
places him beside Dante." Byron himself, dilating on the
strength of his attachment, tells us that he used to coax a
maid to write letters for him, and that when he was
sixteen, on being informed, by his mother, of Mary's
marriage, he nearly fell into convulsions. But in the
history of the calf-loves of poets it is difficult to dis-
tinguish between the imaginative afterthought and the

reality. This equally applies to other recollections of
later years. Moore remarks—"that the charm of scenery,
which derives its chief power from fancy and association,
should be felt at an age when fancy is yet hardly awake
and associations are but few, can with difficulty be conceived." But between the ages of eight and ten, an appreciation of external beauty is sufficiently common. No one
doubts the accuracy of Wordsworth's account, in the
*Prelude* of his early half-sensuous delight in mountain
glory. It is impossible to define the influence of Nature,
either on nations or individuals, or to say beforehand what
selection from his varied surroundings a poet will for
artistic purposes elect to make. Shakespeare rests in
meadows and glades, and leaves to Milton " Teneriffe and
Atlas." Burns, who lived for a considerable part of his
life in daily view of the hills of Arran, never alludes to
them. But, in this respect like Shelley, Byron was
inspired by a passion for the high-places of the earth.
Their shadow is on half his verse. " The loftiest peaks
most wrapt in clouds and snow " perpetually remind him
of one of his constantly recurring refrains,—

> He who surpasses or subdues mankind,
> Must look down on the hate of those below.

In the course of 1796, after an attack of scarlet fever
at Aberdeen he was taken by his mother to Ballater, and
on his recovery spent much of his time in rambling about
the country. "From this period," he says, " I date my love
of mountainous countries. I can never forget the effect,
years afterwards, in England, of the only thing I had
long seen, even in miniature, of a mountain, in the
Malvern Hills. After I returned to Cheltenham I used
to watch them every afternoon, at sunset, with a sensation

which I cannot describe." Elsewhere, in *The Island*
he returns, amid allusions to the Alps and Apennines, to
the friends of his youth :—

> The infant rapture still survived the boy,
> And Lach-na-gair with Ida look'd o'er Troy,
> Mixed Celtic memories with the Phrygian mount,
> And Highland linns with Castalie's clear fount.

The poet, owing to his physical defect, was not a great
climber, and we are informed, on the authority of his
nurse, that he never even scaled the easily attainable
summit of the " steep frowning " hill of which he has
made such effective use.    But the impression of it from a
distance was none the less genuine.    In the midst of a
generous address, in *Don Juan*, to Jeffrey, he again refers
to the same associations with the country of his early
training :—

> But I am half a Scot by birth, and bred
> A whole one ; and my heart flies to my head
> As " Auld Lang Syne " brings Scotland, one and all —
> Scotch plaids, Scotch snoods, the blue hills and clear streams,
> The Dee, the Don, Balgounie's brig's black wall —
> All my boy feelings, all my gentler dreams
> Of what I then dreamt, clothed in their own pall,
> Like Banquo's offspring . . .

Byron's allusions to Scotland are variable and inconsistent.  His satire on her reviewers was sharpened
by the show of national as well as personal antipathy ; and
when, about the time of its production, a young lady
remarked that he had a little of the northern manner of
speech, he burst out "Good God ! I hope not.  I would
rather the whole d—d country was sunk in the sea.    I
the Scotch accent ! "   But in the passage from which we

C

have quoted the swirl of feeling on the other side continues,—

> I rail'd at Scots to show my wrath and wit,
> Which must be own'd was sensitive and surly.
> Yet 'tis in vain such sallies to permit ;
> They cannot quench young feelings, fresh and early.
> I scotch'd, not kill'd, the Scotchman in my blood,
> And love the land of mountain and of flood.

This suggests a few words on a question of more than
local interest.  Byron's most careful biographer has said
of him : " Although on his first expedition to Greece
he was dressed in the tartan of the Gordon clan, yet
the whole bent of his mind, and the character of his
poetry, are anything but Scottish.  Scottish nationality
is tainted with narrow and provincial elements.  Byron's
poetic character, on the other hand, is universal and
cosmopolitan.  He had no attachment to localities, and
never devoted himself to the study of the history of Scotland and its romantic legends."  Somewhat similarly
Thomas Campbell remarks of Burns, " he was the most un-
Scotsmanlike of Scotchmen, having no caution."  Rough
national verdicts are apt to be superficial.  Mr. Leslie Stephen, in a review of Hawthorne, has commented on the
extent to which the nobler qualities and conquering
energy of the English character are hidden, not only
from foreigners, but from ourselves, by the " detestable
lay figure " of John Bull.  In like manner, the obtrusive
type of the " canny Scot " is apt to make critics forget
the hot heart that has marked the early annals of the
country, from the Hebrides to the Borders, with so much
violence, and at the same time has been the source of so
much strong feeling and persistent purpose.  Of late
years, the struggle for existence, the temptations of a too

ambitious and over active people in the race for wealth, and the benumbing effect of the constant profession of beliefs that have ceased to be sincere, have for the most part stifled the fervid fire in calculating prudence. These qualities have been adequately combined in Scott alone, the one massive and complete literary type of his race. Burns, to his ruin, had only the fire : the same is true of Byron, whose genius, in some respects less genuine, was indefinitely and inevitably wider. His intensely susceptible nature took a dye from every scene, city, and society through which he passed ; but to the last he bore with him the marks of a descendant of the Sea-Kings, and of the mad Gordons in whose domains he had first learned to listen to the sound of the "two mighty voices" that haunted and inspired him through life.

In the autumn of 1798 the family, i.e. his mother—who had sold the whole of her household furniture for 75*l*.— with himself, and a maid, set south. The poet's only recorded impression of the journey is a gleam of Loch Leven, to which he refers in one of his latest letters. He never revisited the land of his birth. Our next glimpse of him is on his passing the toll-bar of Newstead. Mrs. Byron asked the old woman who kept it, "Who is the next heir ? " and on her answer "They say it is a little boy who lives at Aberdeen," "This is he, bless him ! " exclaimed the nurse.

Returned to the ancestral Abbey, and finding it half ruined and desolate, they migrated for a time to the neighbouring Nottingham. Here the child's first experience was another course of surgical torture. He was placed under the charge of a quack named Lavender, who rubbed his foot in oil, and screwed it about in wooden machines. This useless treatment is associated

with two characteristic anecdotes. One relates to the
endurance which Byron, on every occasion of mere physical trial, was capable of displaying. Mr. Rogers, a
private tutor, with whom he was reading passages of
Virgil and Cicero, remarked, " It makes me uncomfort-
able, my lord, to see you sitting there in such pain
as I know you must be suffering." " Never mind,
Mr. Rogers," said the child, " you shall not see any
signs of it in me." The other illustrates his precocious
delight in detecting imposture. Having scribbled on
a piece of paper several lines of mere gibberish, he
brought them to Lavender, and gravely asked what
language it was ; and on receiving the answer " It is
Italian," he broke into an exultant laugh at the expense of
his tormentor. Another story survives, of his vindictive
spirit giving birth to his first rhymes. A meddling old
lady, who used to visit his mother and was possessed of a
curious belief in a future transmigration to our satellite—
the bleakness of whose scenery she had not realized—
having given him some cause of offence, he stormed
out to his nurse that he " could not bear the sight of
the witch," and vented his wrath in the couplet,—

> In Nottingham county there lives, at Swan Green,
> As curst an old lady as ever was seen ;
> And when she does die, which I hope will be soon,
> She firmly believes she will go to the moon.

The poet himself dates his " first dash into poetry "
a year later (1800), from his juvenile passion for his
cousin Margaret Parker, whose subsequent death from
an injury caused by a fall he afterwards deplored in a
forgotten elegy. " I do not recollect," he writes through
the transfiguring mists of memory, " anything equal to

the *transparent* beauty of my cousin, or to the sweetness
of her temper, during the short period of our intimacy.
She looked as if she had been made out of a rainbow—all
beauty and peace. My passion had the usual effects upon
me—I could not sleep ; I could not eat ; I could not rest.
It was the texture of my life to think of the time that
must elapse before we could meet again. But I was a fool
then, and not much wiser now." *Sic transit secunda.*

The departure at a somewhat earlier date of May Gray
for her native country, gave rise to evidence of another
kind of affection. On her leaving he presented her with
his first watch, and a miniature by Kay of Edinburgh,
representing him with a bow and arrow in his hand and
a profusion of hair over his shoulders. He continued to
correspond with her at intervals. Byron was always
beloved by his servants. This nurse afterwards married
well, and during her last illness, in 1827, communicated to
her attendant, Dr. Ewing of Aberdeen, recollections of
the poet, from which his biographers have drawn.

In the summer of 1799 he was sent to London, entrusted
to the medical care of Dr. Baillie (brother of Joanna, the
dramatist), and placed in a boarding school at Dulwich,
under the charge of Dr. Glennie. The physician advised
a moderation in athletic sports, which the patient in his
hours of liberty was constantly apt to exceed. The
teacher—who continued to cherish an affectionate remembrance of his pupil, even when he was told, on a visit to
Geneva in 1817, that he ought to have " made a better
boy of him"—testifies to the alacrity with which he
entered on his tasks, his playful good-humour with his
comrades, his reading in history beyond his age, and his
intimate acquaintance with the Scriptures. "In my
study," he states, " he found many books open to him ;

among others, a set of our poets from Chaucer to Churchill,
which I am almost tempted to say he had more than once
perused from beginning to end." One of the books referred to was the *Narrative of the Shipwreck of the* " *Juno,*"
which contains, almost word for word, the account of the
"two fathers," in *Don Juan.* Meanwhile Mrs. Byron,—
whose reduced income had been opportunely augmented
by a grant of a 300*l.* annuity from the Civil List,—
after revisiting Newstead followed her son to London,
and took up her residence in a house in Sloane-terrace.
She was in the habit of having him with her there
from Saturday to Monday, kept him from school for
weeks, introduced him to idle company, and in other
ways was continually hampering his progress.

Byron on his accession to the peerage having become
a ward in Chancery, was handed over by the Court to the
guardianship of Lord Carlisle, nephew of the admiral,
and son of the grand aunt of the poet. Like his mother
this Earl aspired to be a poet, and his tragedy, *The
Father's Revenge,* received some commendation from Dr.
Johnson; but his relations with his illustrious kinsman
were from the first unsatisfactory. In answer to Dr.
Glennie's appeal, he exerted his authority against the
interruptions to his ward's education; but the attempt to
mend matters led to such outrageous exhibitions of
temper that he said to the master, "I can have nothing
more to do with Mrs. Byron ; you must now manage
her as you can." Finally, after two years of work, which
she had done her best to mar, she herself requested his
guardian to have her son removed to a public school,
and accordingly he went to Harrow, where he remained
till the autumn of 1805. The first vacation, in the
summer of 1801, is marked by his visit to Cheltenham,

where his mother, from whom he inherited a fair amount
of Scotch superstition, consulted a fortune-teller, who
said he would be twice married, the second time to a
foreigner.

Harrow was then under the management of Dr. Joseph
Drury, one of the most estimable of its distinguished
head-masters. His account of the first impressions produced by his pupil, and his judicious manner of handling
a sensitive nature, cannot with advantage be condensed.
" Mr. Hanson," he writes, " Lord Byron's solicitor, con-
signed him to my care at the age of thirteen and a half,
with remarks that his education had been neglected ; that
he was ill prepared for a public school ; but that he
thought there was a *cleverness* about him.. After his departure I took my young disciple into my study, and
endeavoured to bring him forward by inquiries as to his
former amusements, employments, and associates, but
with little or no effect, and I soon found that a wild
mountain colt had been submitted to my management.
But there was mind in his eye. In the first place, it was
necessary to attach him to an elder boy ; but the information he received gave him no pleasure when he heard of
the advances of some much younger than himself. This
I discovered, and assured him that he should not be placed
till by diligence he might rank with those of his own age.
His manner and temper soon convinced me that he might
be led by a silken string to a point, rather than a cable :
on that principle I acted."

After a time, Dr. Drury tells us that he waited on
Lord Carlisle, who wished to give some information about
his ward's property and to inquire respecting his abilities,
and continues : " On the former circumstance I made no
remark ; as to the latter I replied, ' He has talents, my

lord, which will add lustre to his rank.' ' Indeed !' said
his lordship, with a degree of surprise that, according to
my feeling, did not express in it all the satisfaction I
expected." With, perhaps, unconscious humour on the
part of the writer, we are left in doubt as to whether
the indifference proceeded from the jealousy that clings to
poetasters, from incredulity, or a feeling that no talent
could add lustre to rank.

In 1804 Byron refers to the antipathy his mother
had to his guardian. Later he expresses gratitude for
some unknown service, in recognition of which the second
edition of the *Hours of Idleness* was dedicated " by his
obliged ward and affectionate kinsman," to Lord Carlisle.
The tribute being coldly received, led to fresh estrange-
ment, and when Byron, on his coming of age, wrote to
remind the Earl of the fact, in expectation of being introduced to the House of Peers, he had for answer a mere
formal statement of its rules. This rebuff affected him
as Addison's praise of Tickell affected Pope, and the following lines, were published in the March of the same
year :—

> Lords too are bards! such things at times befall,
> And 'tis some praise in peers to write at all.
> Yet did or taste or reason sway the times,
> Ah! who would take their titles with their rhymes.
> Roscommon! Sheffield! with your spirits fled,
> No future laurels deck a noble head ;
> No muse will cheer, with renovating smile
> The paralytic puling of Carlisle.

In prose he adds, "If, before I escaped from my teens,
I said anything in favour of his lordship's paper-
books, it was in the way of dutiful dedication, and more
from the advice of others than my own judgment ; and

I seize the first opportunity of pronouncing my sincere
recantation." As was frequently the case with him, he
recanted again. In a letter of 1814 he expressed to Rogers
his regret for his sarcasms ; and in his reference to the
death of the Hon. Frederick Howard, in the third canto
of *Childe Harold,* he tried to make amends in the lines—

> Yet one I would select from that proud throng,
> Partly because they blend me with his line,
> And partly that I did his sire some wrong.

This is all of any interest we know regarding the fitful
connection of the guardian and ward.

Towards Dr. Drury the poet continued through life to
cherish sentiments of gratitude, and always spoke of him
with veneration. " He was," he says, " the best, the
kindest (and yet strict too) friend I ever had ; and I look
on him still as a father, whose warnings I have remembered but too well, though too late, when I have erred,
and whose counsel I have but followed when I have done
well or wisely."

Great educational institutions must consult the greatest
good of the greatest number of common-place minds, by
regulations against which genius is apt to kick ; and
Byron, who was by nature and lack of discipline peculiarly ill fitted to conform to routine, confesses that till the
last year and a half he hated Harrow. He never took
kindly to the studies of the place, and was at no time an
accurate scholar. In the *Bards and Reviewers,* and elsewhere, he evinces considerable familiarity with the leading
authors of antiquity, but it is doubtful whether he was
able to read any of the more difficult of them in the
original. His translations are generally commonplace,
and from the marks on his books he must have often

failed to trust his memory for the meanings of the most
ordinary Greek words. To the well-known passage in
*Childe Harold* on Soracte and the " Latian echoes " he
appends a prose comment, which preserves its interest
as bearing on recent educational controversies :—" I wish
to express that we become tired of the task before
we can comprehend the beauty ; that we learn by rote
before we get by heart ; that the freshness is worn
away, and the future pleasure and advantage deadened
and destroyed, at an age when we can neither feel nor
understand the power of composition, which it requires
an acquaintance with life, as well as Latin and Greek,
to relish or to reason upon . . . . In some parts of
the continent young persons are taught from common
authors, and do not read the best classics till their
maturity."

Comparatively slight stress was then laid on modern
languages. Byron learnt to read French with fluency,
as he certainly made himself familiar with the great
works of the eighteenth century ; but he spoke it with
so little ease or accuracy that the fact was always a
stumbling-block to his meeting Frenchmen abroad. Of
German he had a mere smattering. Italian was the only
language, besides his own, of which he was ever a master.
But the extent and variety of his general reading was
remarkable. His list of books, drawn up in 1807, includes
more history and biography than most men of education
read during a long life ; a fair load of philosophy ; the
poets *en masse ;* among orators, Demosthenes, Cicero, and
Parliamentary debates from the Revolution to the year
1742 ; pretty copious divinity, including Blair, Tillotson,
Hooker, with the characteristic addition—" all very tiresome. I abhor books of religion, though I reverence and

love my God without the blasphemous notions of sectaries."
Lastly, under the head of "Miscellanies" we have *Spectator, Rambler, World*, &c., &c ; among novels, the works
of Cervantes, Fielding, Smollett, Richardson, Mackenzie,
Sterne, Rabelais, and Rousseau.  He recommends Burton's
*Anatomy of Melancholy* as the best storehouse for second-
hand quotations, as Sterne and others have found it, and
tells us that the great part of the books named were
perused before the age of fifteen.  Making allowance for
the fact that most of the poet's autobiographic sketches
are emphatically "*Dichtung und Wahrheit*," we can believe
that he was an omnivorous reader—" I read eating, read
in bed, read when no one else reads "— and, having a
memory only less retentive than Macaulay's, acquired so
much general information as to be suspected of picking it
up from Reviews.  He himself declares that he never
read a Review till he was eighteen years old—when, he
himself wrote one, utterly worthless, on Wordsworth.

At Harrow, Byron proved himself capable of violent
fits of work, but of "few continuous drudgeries."  He
would turn out an unusual number of hexameters, and
again lapse into as much idleness as the teachers would
tolerate.  His forte was in declamation : his attitude
and delivery, and power of extemporizing, surprised
even critical listeners into unguarded praise.  "My
qualities," he says, "were much more oratorical and
martial than poetical ; no one had the least notion that I
should subside into poesy."  Unpopular at first, he began
to like school when he had fought his way to be a
champion, and from his energy in sports more than from
the impression produced by his talents had come to be
recognized as a leader among his fellows.  Unfortunately,
towards the close of his course, in 1805, the headship

of Harrow changed hands. Dr. Drury retired, and was
succeeded by Dr. Butler. This event suggested the lines
beginning,—

> Where are those honours, Ida, once your own,
> When Probus fill'd your magisterial throne ?

The appointment was generally unpopular among the boys,
whose sympathies were enlisted in favour of Henry Drury,
the son of their former master, and Dr. Butler seems for
a time to have had considerable difficulty in maintaining
discipline. Byron, always " famous for rowing," was a
ringleader of the rebellious party, and compared himself
to Tyrtæus. On one occasion he tore down the window
gratings in a room of the school-house, with the remark
that they darkened the hall ; on another he is reported to
have refused a dinner invitation from the master, with
the impertinent remark that he would never think of
asking him in return to dine at Newstead. On the
other hand, he seems to have set limits to the mutiny,
and prevented some of the boys from setting their desks
on fire by pointing to their fathers' names carved on
them. Byron afterwards expressed regret for his rudeness ; but Butler remains in his verse as " Pomposus of
narrow brain, yet of a narrower soul."

Of the poet's free hours, during the last years of his
residence which he refers to as among the happiest of his
life, many were spent in solitary musing by an elm-tree,
near a tomb to which his name has been given—a spot
commanding a far view of London, of Windsor " blos-
somed high in tufted trees," and of the green fields
that stretch between, covered in spring with the white
and red snow of apple blossom. The others were devoted
to the society of his chosen comrades. Byron, if not one

of the safest, was one of the warmest of friends; and he
plucked the more eagerly at the choicest fruit of English
public school and college life, from the feeling he so
pathetically expresses,—

> Is there no cause beyond the common claim,
> Endear'd to all in childhood's very name?
> Ah, sure some stronger impulse vibrates here,
> Which whispers Friendship will be doubly dear
> To one who thus for kindred hearts must roam,
> And seek abroad the love denied at home.
> Those hearts, dear Ida, have I found in thee —
> A home, a world, a paradise to me.

Of his Harrow intimates, the most prominent were the
Duke of Dorset, the poet's favoured fag; Lord Clare (the
Lycus of the *Childish Recollections*); Lord Delawarr
(the Euryalus); John Wingfield (Alonzo), who died at
Coimbra, 1811; Cecil Tattersall (Davus); Edward Noel
Long (Cleon); Wildman, afterwards proprietor of Newstead; and Sir Robert Peel. Of the last, his form-fellow
and most famous of his mates, the story is told of his being
unmercifully beaten for offering resistance to his fag
master, and Byron rushing up to intercede with an offer
to take half the blows. Peel was an exact contemporary,
having been born in the same year, 1788. It has been
remarked that most of the poet's associates were his
juniors, and, less fairly, that he liked to regard them as his
satellites. But even at Dulwich his ostentation of rank
had provoked for him the nickname of "the old English
baron." To Wildman, who, as a senior, had a right of
inflicting chastisement for offences, he said, "I find you
have got Delawarr on your list; pray don't lick him."
"Why not?" was the reply. "Why, I don't know,
except that he is a brother peer." Again, he interfered

with the more effectual arm of physical force to rescue a
junior protégé—lame like himself, and otherwise much
weaker—from the ill-treatment of some hulking tyrant.
"Harness," he said, "if any one bullies you, tell me,
and I'll thrash him if I can;" and he kept his word.
Harness became an accomplished clergyman and minor
poet, and has left some pleasing reminiscences of his
former patron. The prodigy of the school, George
Sinclair, was in the habit of writing the poet's exercises,
and getting his battles fought for him in return. His
bosom friend was Lord Clare. To him his confidences
were most freely given, and his most affectionate verses
addressed. In the characteristic stanzas entitled "L'amitié
est l'amour sans ailes," we feel as if between them the
qualifying phrase might have been omitted : for their
letters, carefully preserved on either side, are a record of
the jealous complaints and the reconciliations of lovers.
In 1821 Byron writes, "I never hear the name Clare
without a beating of the heart even now ; and I write
it with the feelings of 1803-4-5, *ad infinitum.*" At the
same date he says of an accidental meeting : "It anni-
hilated for a moment all the years between the present
time and the days of Harrow. It was a new and inexplicable feeling, like a rising from the grave to me.
Clare too was much agitated—more in appearance than I
was myself—for I could feel his heart beat to his fingers'
ends, unless, indeed, it was the pulse of my own which
made me think so. We were but five minutes together on
the public road, but I hardly recollect an hour of my
existence that could be weighed against them." They
were "all that brothers should be but the name ;" and it is
interesting to trace this relationship between the greatest
genius of the new time and the son of the statesman

who, in the preceding age, stands out serene and strong
amid the swarm of turbulent rioters and ranting orators
by whom he was surrounded and reviled.

Before leaving Harrow the poet had passed through the
experience of a passion of another kind, with a result
that unhappily coloured his life. Accounts differ as to
his first meeting with Mary Ann Chaworth, the heiress
of the family whose estates adjoined his own, and
daughter of the race that had held with his such varied
relations. In one of his letters he dates the introduction
previous to his trip to Cheltenham, but it seems not to
have ripened into intimacy till a later period. Byron,
who had, in the autumn of 1802, visited his mother at
Bath, joined in a masquerade there and attracted attention
by the liveliness of his manners. In the following year
Mrs. Byron again settled at Nottingham, and in the
course of a second and longer visit to her he frequently
passed the night at the Abbey, of which Lord Grey
de Ruthven was then a temporary tenant. This was
the occasion of his renewing his acquaintance with the
Chaworths, who invited him to their seat at Annesley. He
used at first to return every evening to Newstead, giving
the excuse that the family pictures would come down
and take revenge on him for his grand-uncle's deed, a
fancy repeated in the *Siege of Corinth*. Latterly he
consented to stay at Annesley, which thus became his
headquarters during the remainder of the holidays of
1803. The rest of the six weeks were mainly con-
sumed in an excursion to Matlock and Castleton, in
the same companionship. This short period, with the
exception of prologue and epilogue, embraced the whole
story of his first real love. Byron was on this occasion
in earnest; he wished to marry Miss Chaworth, an

event which, he says, would have "joined broad lands,
healed an old feud, and satisfied at least one heart."

The intensity of his passion is suggestively brought
before us in an account of his crossing the Styx of
the Peak cavern, alone with the lady and the Charon
of the boat. In the same passage he informs us that
he had never told his love; but that she had discovered—it is obvious that she never returned—it. We
have another vivid picture of his irritation when she
was waltzing in his presence at Matlock; then an
account of their riding together in the country on their
return to the family residence; again, of his bending over
the piano as she was playing the Welsh air of "Mary
Anne;" and lastly, of his overhearing her heartless
speech to her maid, which first opened his eyes to the
real state of affairs—"Do you think I could care for
that lame boy?"—upon which he rushed out of the house,
and ran, like a hunted creature, to Newstead. Thence he
shortly returned from the rougher school of life to his
haunts and tasks at Harrow. A year later the pair again
met to take farewell, on the hill of Annesley—an incident
he has commemorated in two short stanzas, that have
the sound of a wind moaning over a moor. "I suppose,"
he said, "the next time I see you, you will be Mrs.
Chaworth?" "I hope so," she replied (her betrothed,
Mr. Musters, had agreed to assume her family name).
The announcement of her marriage, which took place
in August, 1805, was made to him by his mother,
with the remark, "I have some news for you. Take
out your handkerchief; you will require it." On hearing what she had to say, with forced calm he turned
the conversation to other subjects; but he was long
haunted by a loss which he has made the theme of

many of his verses.  In 1807 he sent to the lady herself
the lines beginning,—

> O had my fate been join'd with thine.

In the following year he accepted an invitation to dine
at Annesley, and was visibly affected by the sight of the
infant daughter of Mrs. Chaworth, to whom he addressed
a touching congratulation.  Shortly afterwards, when about
to leave England for the first time, he finally addressed
her in the stanzas,—

> 'Tis done, and shivering in the gale,
> The bark unfurls her snowy sail.

Some years later, having an opportunity of revisiting
the family of his successful rival, Mrs. Leigh dissuaded
him.  "Don't go," she said, "for if you do you will certainly fall in love again, and there will be a scene."  The
romance of the story culminates in the famous *Dream*, a
poem of unequal merit, but containing passages of real
pathos, written in the year 1816 at Diodati, as we are
told, amid a flood of tears.

Miss Chaworth's attractions, beyond those of personal
beauty, seem to have been mainly due—a common occur-
rence—to the poet's imagination.  A young lady, two
years his senior, of a lively and volatile temper, she
enjoyed the stolen interviews at the gate between the
grounds, and laughed at the ardent letters, passed through
a confidant, of the still awkward youth whom she
regarded as a boy.  She had no intuition to divine
the presence, or appreciate the worship, of one of the
future master-minds of England, nor any ambition to
ally herself with the wild race of Newstead, and preferred
her hale, commonplace, fox-hunting squire.  "She was

D

the beau ideal," says Byron, in his first accurate prose account of the affair, written 1823, a few days before his departure for Greece, " of all that my youthful fancy could paint of beautiful. And I have taken all my fables about the celestial nature of women from the perfection my imagination created in her. I say created ; for I found her, like the rest of the sex, anything but angelic."

Mrs. Musters (her husband re-asserted his right to his own name) had in the long-run reason to regret her choice. The ill-assorted pair after some unhappy years resolved on separation ; and falling into bad health and worse spirits, the " bright morning star of Annesley " passed under a cloud of mental darkness. She died, in 1832, of fright caused by a Nottingham riot. On the decease of Musters, in 1850, every relic of her ancient family was sold by auction and scattered to the winds.

# CHAPTER III.

In October, 1805, on the advice of Dr. Drury, Byron was removed to Trinity College, Cambridge, and kept up a connexion with the University for less than three years of very irregular attendance, during which we hear nothing of his studies, except the contempt for them expressed in some of the least effective passages of his early satires. He came into residence in bad temper and low spirits. His attachment to Harrow characteristically redoubled as the time drew near to leave it, and his rest was broken "for the last quarter, with counting the hours that remained." He was about to start by himself, with the heavy feeling that he was no longer a boy, and yet, against his choice, for he wished to go to Oxford. The *Hours of Idleness*, the product of this period, are fairly named. He was so idle as regards "problems mathematic," and "barbarous Latin," that it is matter of surprise to learn that he was able to take his degree, as he did in March, 1808.

A good German critic, dwelling on the comparatively narrow range of studies to which the energies of Cambridge were then mainly directed, adds somewhat rashly, that English national literature stands for the most part beyond the range of the academic circle.

This statement is often reiterated with persistent in-
accuracy; but the most casual reference to biography
informs us that at least four-fifths of the leading statesmen, reformers, and philosophers of England, have
been nurtured within the walls of her universities, and
cherished a portion of their spirit. From them have
sprung the intellectual fires that have, at every crisis
of our history, kindled the nation into a new life; from
the age of Wycliffe, through those of Latimer, Locke,
Gibbon, Macaulay, to the present reign of the Physicists,
comparatively few of the motors of their age have been
wholly " without the academic circle." Analysing with
the same view the lives of the British poets of real note
from Barbour to Tennyson, we find the proportion of
University men increases. " Poeta nascitur et fit;" and if
the demands of technical routine have sometimes tended
to stifle, the comparative repose of a seclusion "un-
ravaged" by the fierce activities around it, the habit of
dwelling on the old wisdom and harping on the ancient
strings, is calculated to foster the poetic temper and
enrich its resources. The discouraging effect of a sometimes supercilious and conservative criticism is not an
unmixed evil. The verse-writer who can be snuffed out
by the cavils of a tutorial drone, is a poetaster silenced
for his country's good. It is true, however, that to
original minds, bubbling with spontaneity, or arrogant
with the consciousness of power, the discipline is hard,
and the restraint excessive; and that the men whom
their colleges are most proud to remember, have handled
them severely. Bacon inveighs against the scholastic
trifling of his day; Milton talks of the waste of time on
litigious brawling; Locke mocks at the logic of the
schools; Cowley complains of being taught words, not

things ; Gibbon rejoices over his escape from the port and prejudice of Magdalen ; Wordsworth contemns the " trade in classic niceties," and roves " in magisterial liberty " by the Cam, as afterwards among the hills.

But all those hostile critics owe much to the object of their animadversion. Any schoolboy can refer the preference of Light to Fruit in the *Novum Organum*, half of *Comus* and *Lycidas*, the stately periods of the *Decline and Fall*, and the severe beauties of *Laodamia*, to the better influences of academic training on the minds of their authors. Similarly, the richest pages of Byron's work—from the date of *The Curse of Minerva* to that of the " Isles of Greece "—are brightened by lights and adorned by allusions due to his training, imperfect as it was, on the slopes of Harrow, and the associations fostered during his truant years by the sluggish stream of his "Injusta noverca." At her, however, he continued to rail as late as the publication of *Beppo*, in the 75th and 76th stanzas of which we find another cause of complaint,—

> One hates an author that's all author, fellows
> In foolscap uniforms turn'd up with ink —
> So very anxious, clever, fine, and jealous,
> One don't know what to say to them, or think.

Then, after commending Scott, Rogers, and Moore for being men of the world, he proceeds :—

> But for the children of the "mighty mother's,"
> The would-be wits and can't-be gentlemen,
> I leave them to the daily "Tea is ready,"
> Snug coterie, and literary lady.

This attack, which called forth a counter invective of unusual ferocity from some unknown scribbler, is the expression of a sentiment which, sound enough within

limits, Byron pushed to an extreme. He had a rooted
dislike of professional *littérateurs*, and was always haunted
by a dread that they would claim equality with him on
the common ground of authorship. He aspired through
life to the superiority of a double distinction, that of a
peer among poets, and a poet among peers. In this same
spirit he resented the comparison frequently made between
him and Rousseau, and insisted on points of contrast.
" He had a bad memory, I a good one. He was of the
people ; I of the aristocracy." Byron was capable of
unbending, where the difference of rank was so great that
it could not be ignored. On this principle we may explain his enthusiastic regard for the chorister Eddlestone,
from whom he received the cornelian that is the theme
of some of his verses, and whose untimely death in
1811 he sincerely mourned.

Of his Harrow friends, Harness and Long in due course
followed him to Cambridge, where their common pursuits
were renewed. With the latter, who was drowned in
1809, on a passage to Lisbon with his regiment, he spent
a considerable portion of his time on the Cam, swimming
and diving, in which art they were so expert as to pick
up eggs, plates, thimbles, and coins from a depth of
fourteen feet—incidents recalled to the poet's mind by
reading Milton's invocation to Sabrina. During the
same period he distinguished himself at cricket, as in
boxing, riding, and shooting. Of his skill as a rider there are
various accounts. He was an undoubted marksman, and his
habit of carrying about pistols, and use of them wherever he
went, was often a source of annoyance and alarm. He professed a theoretical objection to duelling, but was as ready
to take a challenge as Scott, and more ready to send one.

Regarding the masters and professors of Cambridge,

Byron has little to say.  His own tutor, Tavell, appears
pleasantly enough in his verse, and he commends
the head of his college, Dr. Lort Mansel, for dignified
demeanour in his office, and a past reputation for convivial
wit.  His attentions to Professor Hailstone at Harrow-
gate were graciously offered and received ; but in a
letter to Murray he gives a graphically abusive account
of Porson, " hiccuping Greek like a Helot" in his cups.
The poet was first introduced at Cambridge to a brilliant
circle of contemporaries, whose talents or attainments soon
made them more or less conspicuous, and most of whom
are interesting on their own account as well as from their
connection with the subsequent phases of his career.  By
common consent Charles Skinner Matthews, son of the
member for Herefordshire, 1802-6, was the most remarkable of the group.  Distinguished alike for scholarship,
physical and mental courage, subtlety of thought, humour
of fancy, and fascinations of character, this young man
seems to have made an impression on the undergraduates
of his own, similar to that left by Charles Austin on
those of a later generation.  The loss of this friend
Byron always regarded as an incalculable calamity.
In a note to *Childe Harold* he writes, " I should
have ventured on a verse to the memory of Matthews,
were he not too much above all praise of mine.  His
powers of mind shown in the attainment of greater
honours against the ablest candidates, than those of any
graduate on record at Cambridge, have sufficiently established his fame on the spot where it was acquired ; while
his softer qualities live in the recollection of friends, who
loved him too well to envy his superiority."  He was
drowned when bathing alone among the reeds of the Cam,
in the summer of 1811.

In a letter written from Ravenna in 1820, Byron, in answer to a request for contributions to a proposed memoir, introduces into his notes much autobiographical matter. In reference to a joint visit to Newstead, he writes: "Matthews and myself had travelled down from London together, talking all the way incessantly upon one single topic. When we got to Loughborough, I know not what chasm had made us diverge for a moment to some other subject, at which he was indignant. 'Come,' said he, 'don't let us break through; let us go on as we began, to our journey's end;' and so he continued, and was as entertaining as ever to the very end. He had previously occupied, during my year's absence from Cambridge, my rooms in Trinity, with the furniture; and Jones (the gyp), in his odd way had said, in putting him in, 'Mr. Matthews, I recommend to your attention not to damage any of the movables, for Lord Byron, sir, is a young man of *tumultuous passions.*' Matthews was delighted with this, and whenever anybody came to visit him, begged them to handle the very door with caution, and used to repeat Jones's admonition in his tone and manner. . . . He had the same droll sardonic way about everything. A wild Irishman, named F., one evening beginning to say something at a large supper, Matthews roared 'Silence!' and then pointing to F., cried out, in the words of the oracle, 'Orson is endowed with reason.' When Sir Henry Smith was expelled from Cambridge for a row with a tradesman named 'Hiron,' Matthews solaced himself with shouting under Hiron's windows every evening —

> Ah me! what perils do environ
> The man who meddles with hot Hiron!

He was also of that band of scoffers who used to rouse
Lort Mansel from his slumbers in the lodge of Trinity;
and when he appeared at the window, foaming with wrath,
and crying out, "I know you, gentlemen ; I know you!"
were wont to reply, "We beseech thee to hear us, good
Lort. Good Lort, deliver us ! "

The whole letter, written in the poet's mature and natural
style, gives a vivid picture of the social life and surroundings of his Cambridge days : how much of the set and
sententious moralizing of some of his formal biographers
might we not have spared, for a report of the conversation
on the road from London to Newstead. Of the others
gathered round the same centre, Scrope Davies enlisted
the largest share of Byron's affections. To him he wrote
after the catastrophe :—" Come to me, Scrope ; I am
almost desolate—left alone in the world. I had but you,
and H., and M., and let me enjoy the survivors while I
can." Later he says, " Matthews, Davies, Hobhouse, and
myself formed a coterie of our own. Davies has always
beaten us all in the war of words, and by colloquial
powers at once delighted and kept us in order ; even M.
yielded to the dashing vivacity of S. D." The last is
everywhere commended for the brilliancy of his wit and
repartee : he was never afraid to speak the truth. Once
when the poet in one of his fits of petulance exclaimed,
intending to produce a terrible impression, "I shall go
*mad !* " Davies calmly and cuttingly observed, " It is much
more like silliness than madness ! " He was the only
man who ever laid Byron under any serious pecuniary
obligation, having lent him 4800*l.* in some time of strait.
This was repaid on March 27, 1814, when the pair sat up
over champagne and claret from six till midnight, after
which " Scrope could not be got into the carriage on the

way home, but remained tipsy and pious on his knees."
Davies was much disconcerted at the influence which the
sceptical opinions of Matthews threatened to exercise over
Byron's mind. The fourth of this quadrangle of amity
was John Cam Hobhouse, afterwards Lord Broughton,
the steadfast friend of the poet's whole life, the companion of his travels, the witness of his marriage, the
executor of his will, the zealous guardian and vindicator
of his fame. His ability is abundantly attested by the
impression he left on his contemporaries, his published
description of the Pilgrimage, and subsequent literary
and political career. Byron bears witness to the warmth
of his affections, and the charms of his conversation,
and to the candour which, as he confessed to Lady Blessington, sometimes tried his patience. There is little
doubt that they had some misunderstanding when travelling together, but it was a passing cloud. Eighteen
months after his return the poet admits that Hobhouse
was his best friend ; and when he unexpectedly walked
up the stairs of the Palazzo Lanfranchi, at Pisa, Madame
Guiccioli informs us that Byron was seized with such violent
emotion, and so extreme an excess of joy, that it seemed
to take away his strength, and he was forced to sit down
in tears.

On the edge of this inner circle, and in many respects
associated with it, was the Rev. Francis Hodgson, a ripe
scholar, good translator, a sound critic, a fluent writer
of graceful verse, and a large-hearted divine, whose correspondence, recently edited with a connecting narrative
by his son, has thrown light on disputed passages of
Lord Byron's life. The views entertained by the friends
on literary matters were almost identical ; they both
fought under the standards of the classic school ; they

resented the same criticisms, they applauded the same successes, and were bound together by the strong tie of mutual admiration. Byron commends Hodgson's verses, and encourages him to write; Hodgson recognizes in the *Bards and Reviewers* and the early cantos of *Childe Harold* the promise of *Manfred* and *Cain*. Among the associates who strove to bring the poet back to the anchorage of fixed belief, and to wean him from the error of his thoughts, Francis Hodgson was the most charitable, and therefore the most judicious. That his cautions and exhortations were never stultified by pedantry or excessive dogmatism, is apparent from the frank and unguarded answers which they called forth. In several, which are preserved, and some for the first time reproduced in the recently-published Memoir, we are struck by the mixture of audacity and superficial dogmatism, sometimes amounting to effrontery, that is apt to characterize the negations of a youthful sceptic. In September, 1811, Byron writes from Newstead :—" I will have nothing to do with your immortality; we are miserable enough in this life, without the absurdity of speculating upon another. Christ came to save men, but a good Pagan will go to heaven, and a bad Nazarene to hell. I am no Platonist, I am nothing at all; but I would sooner be a Paulician, Manichean, Spinozist, Gentile, Pyrrhonian, Zoroastrian, than one of the seventy-two villainous sects who are tearing each other to pieces for the love of the Lord and hatred of each other. I will bring ten Mussulmen, shall shame you all in good will towards men and prayer to God." On a similar outburst in verse, the Rev. F. Hodgson comments with a sweet humanity, "The poor dear soul meant nothing of this." Elsewhere the poet writes, "I have read Watson to Gibbon.

He proves nothing ; so I am where I was, verging towards Spinoza ; and yet it is a gloomy creed ; and I want a better ; but there is something pagan in me that I cannot shake off. *In short, I deny nothing, but doubt everything.*" But his early attitude on matters of religion is best set forth in a letter to Gifford, of 1813, in which he says, " I am no bigot to infidelity, and did not expect that because I doubted the immortality of man I should be charged with denying the existence of a God. It was the comparative insignificance of ourselves and our world, when placed in comparison of the mighty whole of which man is an atom, that first led me to imagine that our pretensions to eternity might be overrated. This, and being early disgusted with a Calvinistic Scotch school, where I was cudgelled to church for the first ten years of my life, afflicted me with this malady ; for, after all, it is, I believe, a disease of the mind, as much as other kinds of hypochondria."

Hodgson was a type of friendly forbearance and loyal attachment, which had for their return a perfect open-heartedness in his correspondent. To no one did the poet more freely abuse himself ; to no one did he indulge in more reckless sallies of humour ; to no one did he more readily betray his little conceits. From him Byron sought and received advice, and he owed to him the prevention of what might have been a most foolish and disastrous encounter. On the other hand, the clergyman was the recipient of one of the poet's many single-hearted acts of munificence —a gift of 1000*l.*, to pay off debts to which he had been left heir. In a letter to his uncle, the former gratefully alludes to this generosity : " Oh, if you knew the exultation of heart, aye, and of head to, I feel at being free from those depressing embarrassments, you would,

as I do, bless my dearest friend and brother, Byron."
The whole transaction is a pleasing record of a benefit that
was neither sooner nor later resented by the receiver.

Among other associates of the same group should be mentioned Henry Drury—long Hodgson's intimate friend, and
ultimately his brother-in-law, to whom many of Byron's
first series of letters from abroad are addressed—and
Robert Charles Dallas, a name surrounded with various
associations, who played a not insignificant part in
Byron's history, and, after his death, helped to swell
the throng of his annotators. This gentleman, a connexion by marriage, and author of some now forgotten
novels, first made acquaintance with the poet in London
early in 1808, when we have two letters from Byron,
in answer to some compliment on his early volume, in
which, though addressing his correspondent merely as
' Sir,' his flippancy and habit of boasting of excessive bad-
ness reach an absurd climax.

Meanwhile, during the intervals of his attendance at
college, Byron had made other friends.  His vacations
were divided between London and Southwell, a small
town on the road from Mansfield and Newark, once a
refuge of Charles I., and still adorned by an old Norman
minster.  Here Mrs. Byron for several summer seasons
took up her abode, and was frequently joined by her son.
He was introduced to John Pigot, a medical student of
Edinburgh, and his sister Elizabeth, both endowed with
talents above the average, and keenly interested in literary
pursuits, to whom a number of his letters are addressed ;
also to the Rev. J. T. Becher, author of a treatise on the
state of the poor, to whom he was indebted for encouragement and counsel.  The poet often rails at the
place, which he found dull in comparison with Cambridge

and London; writing from the latter, in 1807 : "O Southwell, how I rejoice to have left thee! and how I curse the heavy hours I dragged along for so many months among the Mohawks who inhabit your kraals!" and adding, that his sole satisfaction during his residence there was having pared off some pounds of flesh. Notwithstanding, in the small but select society of this inland watering-place he passed on the whole a pleasant time— listening to the music of the simple ballads in which he delighted, taking part in the performances of the local theatre, making excursions, and writing verses. This otherwise quiet time was disturbed by exhibitions of violence on the part of Mrs. Byron, which suggest the idea of insanity. After one more outrageous than usual, both mother and son are said to have gone to the neighbouring apothecary, each to request him not to supply the other with poison. On a later occasion, when he had been meeting her bursts of rage with stubborn mockery, she flung a poker at his head, and narrowly missed her aim. Upon this he took flight to London, and his Hydra or Alecto, as he calls her, followed : on their meeting a truce was patched, and they withdrew in opposite directions, she back to Southwell, he to refresh himself on the Sussex coast, till in the August of the same year (1806) he again rejoined her. Shortly afterwards we have from Pigot a description of a trip to Harrogate, when his lordship's favourite Newfoundland, Boatswain, whose relation to his master recalls that of Bounce to Pope, or Maida to Scott, sat on the box.

In November Byron printed for private circulation the first issue of his juvenile poems. Mr. Becher having called his attention to one which he thought objectionable, the impression was destroyed; and the author set to work upon another, which, at once weeded and amplified, saw the light in January, 1807. He sent copies, under the title of *Juvenilia*, to several of his friends, and among others to Henry Mackenzie (the Man of Feeling), and to Fraser Tytler, Lord Woodhouselee. Encouraged by their favourable notices, he determined to appeal to a wider audience, and in March, 1807, the *Hours of Idleness*, still proceeding from the local press at Newark, were given to the world. In June we find the poet again writing from his college rooms, dwelling with boyish detail on his growth in height and reduction in girth, his late hours and heavy potations, his comrades, and the prospects of his book. From July to September he dates from London, excited by the praises of some now obscure magazine, and planning a journey to the Hebrides. In October he is again settled at Cambridge, and in a letter to Miss Pigot, makes a humorous reference to one of his fantastic freaks : " I have got a new friend, the finest in the world—a *tame bear*. When I brought him here, they asked me what I meant to do with him, and my reply was, ' He should sit for a fellowship.' This answer delighted them not." The greater part of the spring and summer of 1808 was spent at Dorant's Hotel, Albemarle Street. Left to himself, he seems during this period for the first time to have freely indulged in dissipations, which are in most lives more or less carefully concealed. But Byron, with almost unparalleled folly, was perpetually taking the public into his confidence, and all his " sins of blood," with the strange additions of an imaginative effrontery, have been thrust before us in a manner which even Théophile Gautier might have thought indelicate. Nature and circumstances conspired to the result. With passions which

he is fond of comparing to the fires of Vesuvius and
Hecla, he was, on his entrance into a social life which his
rank helped to surround with temptations, unconscious of
any sufficient motive for resisting them ; he had no one
to restrain him from the whim of the moment, or with
sufficient authority to give him effective advice.   A
temperament of general despondency, relieved by reckless outbursts of animal spirits, is the least favourable to habitual self-control.   The melancholy of Byron
was not of the pensive and innocent kind attributed
to Cowley, rather that of the μελαγχολικοί of whom
Aristotle asserts, with profound psychological or physio-
logical intuition, that they are ἀεὶ ἐν σφοδρᾷ ὀρέξει.
The absurdity of Mr. Moore's frequent declaration, that
all great poets are inly wrapt in perpetual gloom, is only
to be excused by the modesty which, in the saying so,
obviously excludes himself from the list.   But it is true
that anomalous energies are sources of incessant irritation
to their possessor, until they have found their proper vent
in the free exercise of his highest faculties.   Byron had
not yet done this, when he was rushing about between
London, Brighton, Cambridge, and Newstead—shooting,
gambling, swimming, alternately drinking deep and
trying to starve himself into elegance, green-room hunt-
ing, travelling with disguised companions,[1] patronizing
D'Egville the dancing-master, Grimaldi the clown, and
taking lessons from Mr. Jackson, the distinguished professor of pugilism, to whom he afterwards affectionately

---

[1] In reference to one of these, see an interesting letter from Mr.
Minto to the *Athenæum* in the year 1876, in which, with considerable though not conclusive ingenuity, he endeavours to
identify the girl with " Thyrza " and with "Astarté," whom he
regards as the same person.

refers as his " old friend and corporeal pastor and master."
There is no inducement to dwell on amours devoid of
romance, further than to remember that they never
trenched on what the common code of the fashionable
world terms dishonour. We may believe the poet's later
assertion, backed by want of evidence to the contrary,
that he had never been the first means of leading any one
astray—a fact perhaps worthy the attention of those
moral worshippers of Goethe and Burns who hiss at Lord
Byron's name.

Though much of this year of his life was passed
unprofitably, from it dates the impulse that provoked
him to put forth his powers. The *Edinburgh*, with the
attack on the *Hours of Idleness*, appeared in March, 1808.
This production, by Lord Brougham, is a specimen of the
tomahawk style of criticism prevalent in the early years of
the century, in which the main motive of the critic was, not
to deal fairly with his author, but to acquire for himself
an easy reputation for cleverness, by a series of smart con-
temptuous sentences. Taken separately, the strictures of
the *Edinburgh* are sufficiently just, and the passages
quoted for censure are all bad. Byron's genius as a poet
was not remarkably precocious. The *Hours of Idleness*
seldom rise, either in thought or expression, very far
above the average level of juvenile verse ; many of the
pieces in the collection are weak imitations, or commonplace descriptions : others suggested by circumstances of
local or temporary interest, had served their turn before
coming into print. Their prevailing sentiment is an
affectation of misanthropy, conveyed in such lines as
these :—

> Weary of love, of life, devour'd with spleen,
> I rest, a perfect Timon, not nineteen.

E

This mawkish element unfortunately survives in much
of the author's later verse. But even in this volume
there are indications of force, and command. The *Prayer
of Nature* indeed, though previously written, was not
included in the edition before the notice of the critic ; but
the sound of *Loch-na-Gair* and some of the stanzas on
*Newstead* ought to have saved him from the mistake of his
impudent advice. The poet, who through life waited with
feverish anxiety for every verdict on his work, is reported
after reading the review to have looked like a man about to
send a challenge. In the midst of a transparent show of
indifference, he confesses to have drunk three bottles of
claret on the evening of its appearance. But the wound
did not mortify into torpor ; the Sea-Kings' blood stood
him in good stead, and he was not long in collecting
his strength for the panther-like spring, which, gaining
strength by its delay, twelve months later made it impossible for him to be contemned.

The last months of the year he spent at Newstead,
vacated by the tenant, who had left the building in the
tumble-down condition in which he found it. Byron
was, by his own acknowledgment, at this time, "heavily
dipped," generosities having combined with selfish ex-
travagances to the result ; he had no funds to subject the
place to anything like a thorough repair, but he busied
himself in arranging a few of the rooms for his own
present and his mother's after use. About this date he
writes to her, beginning in his usual style, "Dear Madam,"
saying he has as yet no rooms ready for her reception,
but that on his departure she shall be tenant till his
return. During this interval he was studying Pope, and
carefully maturing his own Satire. In November the
dog Boatswain died in a fit of madness. The event

called forth the famous burst of misanthropic verse, ending with the couplet,—

> To mark a friend's remains these stones arise;
> I never knew but *one*, and *here* he lies ;—

and the inscription on the monument that still remains in the gardens of Newstead,—

> Near this spot
> Are deposited the remains of one
> Who possessed Beauty without Vanity,
> Strength without Insolence,
> Courage without Ferocity,
> And all the virtues of Man without his Vices.
> This Praise, which would be unmeaning Flattery
> If inscribed over human ashes,
> Is but a just tribute to the Memory of
> Boatswain, a Dog,
> Who was born at Newfoundland, May, 1803,
> And died at Newstead Abbey, November 18, 1808.

On January 22, 1809, his lordship's coming of age was celebrated with festivities, curtailed of their proportions by his limited means. Early in spring he paid a visit to London, bringing the proof of his satire to the publisher, Cawthorne. From St. James's Street he writes to Mrs. Byron, on the death of Lord Falkland, who had been killed in a duel, and expresses a sympathy for his family, left in destitute circumstances, whom he proceeded to relieve with a generosity only equalled by the delicacy of the manner in which it was shown. Referring to his own embarrassment, he proceeds in the expression of a resolve, often repeated, " Come what may, Newstead and I stand or fall together. I have now lived on the spot—I have fixed my heart on it ; and no pressure, present or future, shall induce me to barter the last vestige of our inheritance." He was building false hopes on the result of the suit for the Rochdale property, which, being dragged from court to court, involved him in heavy expenses, with no satisfactory result. He took his seat in the House of Lords on the 13th of March, and Mr. Dallas, who accompanied him to the bar of the House, has left an account of his somewhat unfortunate demeanour.

"His countenance, paler than usual, showed that his mind was agitated, and that he was thinking of the nobleman to whom he had once looked for a hand and countenance in his introduction. There were very few persons in the House. Lord Eldon was going through some ordinary business. When Lord Byron had taken the oaths, the Chancellor quitted his seat, and went towards him with a smile, putting out his hand warmly to welcome him; and, though I did not catch the words, I saw that he paid him some compliment. This was all thrown away upon Lord Byron, who made a stiff bow, and put the tips of his fingers into the Chancellor's hand. The Chancellor did not press a welcome so received, but resumed his seat; while Lord Byron carelessly seated himself for a few minutes on one of the empty benches to the left of the throne, usually occupied by the lords in Opposition. When, on his joining me, I expressed what I had felt, he said ' If I had shaken hands heartily, he would have set me down for one of his party; but I will have nothing to do with them on either side. I have taken my seat, and now I will go abroad.' "

A few days later the *English Bards and Scotch Reviewers* appeared before the public. The first anonymous edition was exhausted in a month; a second, to which the author gave his name, quickly followed. He was wont at a later date to disparage this production, and frequently recanted many of his verdicts in marginal notes.  Several, indeed, seem to have been dictated by feelings so transitory, that in the course of the correction of proof blame was turned into praise, and praise into blame ; i.e. he wrote in MS. before he met the agreeable author,—

> I leave topography to coxcomb Gell ;

we have his second thought in the first edition, before he saw the Troad,—

> I leave topography to classic Gell ;

and his third, half way in censure, in the fifth,—

> I leave topography to rapid Gell.

Of such materials are literary judgments made !

The success of Byron's satire was due to the fact of its being the only good thing of its kind since Churchill,—for in the *Baviad* and *Mæviad* only butterflies were broken upon the wheel—and to its being the first promise of a new power.  The *Bards and Reviewers* also enlisted sympathy, from its vigorous attack upon the critics who had hitherto assumed the prerogative of attack.  Jeffrey and Brougham were seethed in their own milk ; and outsiders, whose credentials were still being examined, as Moore and Campbell, came in for their share of vigorous vituperation.  The Lakers fared worst of all.  It was the beginning of the author's lifelong war, only once relaxed, with Southey.  Wordsworth —though against this passage is written " unjust," a concession not much sooner made than withdrawn,—is dubbed an idiot, who—

> Both by precept and example shows,
> That prose is verse and verse is only prose ;

and Coleridge, a baby,—

> To turgid ode and tumid stanza dear.

The lines ridiculing the encounter between Jeffrey and
Moore, are a fair specimen of the accuracy with which the
author had caught the ring of Pope's antithesis :—

> The surly Tolbooth scarcely kept her place.
> The Tolbooth felt—for marble sometimes can,
> On such occasions, feel as much as man—
> The Tolbooth felt defrauded of her charms,
> If Jeffrey died, except within her arms.

Meanwhile Byron had again retired to Newstead, where
he invited some choice spirits to hold a few weeks of
farewell revel.   Matthews, one of these, gives an
account of the place, and the time they spent there
—entering the mansion between a bear and a wolf, amid
a salvo of pistol-shots ; sitting up to all hours, talking
politics, philosophy, poetry ; hearing stories of the dead
lords, and the ghost of the Black Brother ; drinking their
wine out of the skull cup which the owner had made
out of the cranium of some old monk dug up in the
garden ; breakfasting at two, then reading, fencing, riding,
cricketting, sailing on the lake, and playing with the
bear or teasing the wolf.   The party broke up without
having made themselves responsible for any of the orgies
of which Childe Harold raves, and which Dallas in good
earnest accepts as veracious, when the poet and his friend
Hobhouse started for Falmouth, on their way " *outre mer*."

# CHAPTER IV.

THERE is no romance of Munchausen or Dumas more marvellous than the adventures attributed to Lord Byron abroad. Attached to his first expedition are a series of narratives, by professing eye-witnesses, of his intrigues, encounters, acts of diablerie and of munificence, in particular of his roaming about the isles of Greece and taking possession of one of them, which have all the same relation to reality as the *Arabian Nights* to the actual reign of Haroun Al Raschid.[1]

Byron had far more than an average share of the *émigré* spirit, the counterpoise in the English race of their otherwise arrogant isolation. He held with Wilhelm Meister—

> To give space for wandering is it,
> That the earth was made so wide.

and wrote to his mother from Athens : " I am so convinced of the advantages of looking at mankind, instead of reading about them, and the bitter effects of staying at home with all the narrow prejudices of an islander, that I think

[1] Those who wish to read them are referred to the large three volumes—published in 1825, by Mr. Iley, Portman Square—of anonymous authorship.

there should be a law amongst us to send our young men abroad for a term, among the few allies our wars have left us."

On June 11th, having borrowed money at heavy interest, and stored his mind with information about Persia and India, the contemplated but unattained goal of his travels, he left London, accompanied by his friend Hobhouse, Fletcher his valet, Joe Murray his old butler, and Robert Rushton the son of one of his tenants, supposed to be represented by the Page in *Childe Harold*. The two latter, the one on account of his age, the other from his health breaking down, he sent back to England from Gibraltar.

Becalmed for some days at Falmouth, a town which he describes as "full of Quakers and salt fish," he despatched letters to his mother, Drury, and Hodgson, exhibiting the changing moods of his mind. Smarting under a slight he had received at parting from a school-companion, who had excused himself from a farewell meeting on the plea that he had to go shopping, he at one moment talks of his desolation, and says that, "leaving England without regret," he has thought of entering the Turkish service ; in the next, especially in the stanzas to Hodgson, he runs off into a strain of boisterous buffoonery. On the 2nd of July, the packet, by which he was bound, sailed for Lisbon and arrived there about the middle of the month, when the English fleet was anchored in the Tagus. The poet in some of his stanzas has described the fine view of the port and the disconsolate dirtiness of the city itself, the streets of which were at that time rendered dangerous by the frequency of religious and political assassinations. Nothing else remains of his sojourn to interest us, save the statement of Mr. Hob-

house, that his friend made a more perilous, though less
celebrated, achievement by water than his crossing the
Hellespont, in swimming from old Lisbon to Belem Castle.
Byron praises the neighbouring Cintra, as "the most
beautiful village in the world," though he joins with
Wordsworth in heaping anathemas on the Convention, and
extols the grandeur of Mafra, the Escurial of Portugal, in
the convent of which a monk, showing the traveller a large
library, asked if the English had any books in their
country. Despatching his baggage and servants by sea
to Gibraltar, he and his friend started on horseback
through the south-west of Spain. Their first resting-
place, after a ride of 400 miles, performed at an
average rate of seventy in the twenty-four hours, was
Seville, where they lodged for three days in the house of
two ladies, to whose attractions, as well as the fascination
he seems to have exerted over them, the poet somewhat
garrulously refers. Here, too, he saw, parading on the
Prado, the famous *Maid of Saragossa*, whom he celebrates
in his equally famous stanzas (*Childe Harold*, I., 54—58).
Of Cadiz, the next stage, he writes with enthusiasm
as a modern Cythera, describing the bull fights in his
verse, and the beauties in glowing prose. The belles of
this city, he says, are the Lancashire witches of Spain ;
and by reason of them, rather than the sea-shore or the
Sierra Morena, "sweet Cadiz is the first spot in the
creation." Hence, by an English frigate, they sailed to
Gibraltar, for which place he has nothing but curses.
Byron had no sympathy with the ordinary forms of
British patriotism, and in our great struggle with the
tyranny of the First Empire, he may almost be said to
have sympathized with Napoleon.

The ship stopped at Cagliari in Sardinia, and again at

Girgenti on the Sicilian coast. Arriving at Malta, they
halted there for three weeks—time enough to establish a
sentimental, though Platonic, flirtation with Mrs. Spencer
Smith, wife of our minister at Constantinople, sister-in-
law of the famous admiral, and the heroine of some ex-
citing adventures. She is the "Florence" of *Childe
Harold*, and is afterwards addressed in some of the most
graceful verses of his cavalier minstrelsy—

> Do thou, amidst the fair white walls,
>   If Cadiz yet be free,
> At times from out her latticed halls
>   Look o'er the dark blue sea—
> Then think upon Calypso's isles,
>   Endear'd by days gone by,—
> To others give a thousand smiles,
>   To me a single sigh.

The only other adventure of the visit is Byron's quarrel
with an officer, on some unrecorded ground, which Hobhouse tells us nearly resulted in a duel. The friends left
Malta on September 29th, in the war-ship "Spider," and
after anchoring off Patras, and spending a few hours on
shore, they skirted the coast of Acarnania, in view of
localities—as Ithaca, the Leucadian rock, and Actium
—whose classic memories filtered through the poet's mind
and found a place in his masterpieces. Landing at
Previsa, they started on a tour through Albania,—

> O'er many a mount sublime,
> Through lands scarce noticed in historic tales.

Byron was deeply impressed by the beauty of the
scenery, and the half-savage independence of the people,
described as "always strutting about with slow dignity,

though in rags." In October we find him with his companions at Janina, hospitably entertained by order of
Ali Pasha, the famous Albanian Turk, bandit, and despot,
then engaged in besieging Ibrahim in Illyria.    They
proceeded on their way by "bleak Pindus," Acherusia's
lake, and Zitza, with its monastery door battered by
robbers. Before reaching the latter place, they encountered
a terrific thunderstorm, in the midst of which they
separated, and Byron's detachment lost its way for nine
hours, during which he composed the verses to Florence,
quoted above.

Some days later they together arrived at Tepelleni, and
were there received by Ali Pasha in person.    The scene on
entering the town is described as recalling  Scott's Brank-
some Castle and  the feudal system ; and the introduction
to Ali,  who sat for some of the traits of the poet's corsairs,
—is graphically  reproduced  in a letter to Mrs. Byron.
" His first  question was, why at so early an age I left my
country, and without a ' lala,' or nurse ?  He then said
the English minister had told him I was of a great family,
and desired his respects to my mother, which I now present to you (date, November 12th). He said he was certain
I was a man of birth, because I had small ears, curling hair,
and little white hands.    He told me to consider him as a
father whilst I was in Turkey, and said he looked on me as
his son.    Indeed  he treated me like a child, sending me
almonds, fruit, and sweetmeats, twenty times a  day."
Byron shortly afterwards discovered his host to be a
poisoner and an assassin.   " Two days ago," he proceeds
in a passage which illustrates his character and a common
experience, " I was nearly lost in a Turkish ship-of-war,
owing to the ignorance of the captain and crew.   Fletcher
yelled after his wife ; the Greeks called on all the saints,

the Mussulmen on Alla ; the captain burst into tears and
ran below deck, telling us to call on God.  The sails were
split, the mainyard shivered, the wind blowing fresh,
the night setting in ; and all our chance was to make
for Corfu — or, as F. pathetically called it, 'a watery
grave.'  I did what I could to console him, but finding
him incorrigible, wrapped myself in my Albanian capote,
and lay down on the deck to wait the worst."  Unable
from his lameness, says Hobhouse, to be of any assistance,
he in a short time was found amid the trembling sailors,
fast asleep.  They got back to the coast of Suli, and
shortly afterwards started through Acarnania and Ætolia
for the Morea, again rejoicing in the wild scenery and the
apparently kindred spirits of the wild men among whom
they passed.  Byron was especially fascinated by the fire-
light dance and song of the robber band, which he
describes and reproduces in *Childe Harold*.  On the 21st
of November he reached Mesolonghi, where, fifteen years
later, he died.  Here he dismissed most of his escort,
proceeded to Patras, and on to Vostizza, caught sight of
Parnassus, and accepted a flight of eagles near Delphi
as a favouring sign of Apollo.  " The last bird," he writes,
" I ever fired at was an eaglet on the shore of the Gulf of
Lepanto.  It was only wounded and I tried to save it—
the eye was so bright.  But it pined and died in a few
days : and I never did since, and never will, attempt the
life of another bird."  From Livadia the travellers proceeded to Thebes, visited the cave of Trophonius, Diana's
fountain, the so-called ruins of Pindar's house, and the field
of Cheronea, crossed Cithæron, and on Christmas, 1809,
arrived before the defile, near the ruins of Phyle, where,
he had his first glimpse of Athens, which evoked the
famous lines :—

Ancient of days, august Athena! where,
Where are thy men of might ? thy grand in soul ?
Gone, glimmering through the dreams of things that were.
First in the race that led to glory's goal,
They won, and pass'd away : is this the whole —
A schoolboy's tale, the wonder of an hour ?

After which he reverts to his perpetually recurring moral,
"Men come and go ; but the hills, and waves, and skies,
and stars, endure "—

Apollo still thy long, long summer gilds ;
Still in his beam Mendeli's marbles glare ;
Art, glory, freedom fail—but nature still is fair.

The duration of Lord Byron's first visit to Athens was
about three months, and it was varied by excursions to
different parts of Attica; Eleusis, Hymettus, Cape Colonna,
Sunium, the scene of Falconer's shipwreck, the Colonos
of Œdipus, and Marathon, the plain of which is said to
have been placed at his disposal for about the same sum
that thirty years later an American volunteered to give
for the bark with his name on the tree at Newstead.
Byron had a poor opinion of the modern Athenians, who
seem to have at this period done their best to justify
the Roman satirist.  He found them superficial, cunning,
and false ; but, with generous historic insight, he says
that no nation in like circumstances would have been
much better ; that they had the vices of ages of slavery,
from which it would require ages of freedom to emancipate
them.

In the Greek capital he lodged at the house of a
respectable lady, widow of an English vice-consul, who
had three daughters, the eldest of whom, Theresa, acquired
an innocent and enviable fame as the Maid of Athens,
without the dangerous glory of having taken any very

firm hold of the heart that she was asked to return. A more
solid passion was the poet's genuine indignation on the
"lifting," in Border· phrase, of the marbles from the
Parthenon, and their being taken to England by order of
Lord Elgin. Byron never wrote anything more sincere
than the *Curse of Minerva;* and he has recorded few
incidents more pathetic than that of the old Greek who,
when the last stone was removed for exportation, shed
tears, and said "τέλος!" The question is still an open
one of ethics. There are few Englishmen of the higher
rank who do not hold London in the right hand as barely
balanced by the rest of the world in the left; a judgment
in which we can hardly expect Romans, Parisians, and
Athenians to concur. On the other hand, the marbles
were mouldering at Athens, and they are preserved, like
ginger, in the British Museum.

Among the adventures of this period are an expedition
across the Ilissus to some caves near Kharyati, in which
the travellers were by accident nearly entombed; another
to Pentelicus, where they tried to carve their names
on the marble rock; and a third to the environs of the
Piræus in the evening light. Early in March the con-
venient departure of an English sloop-of-war induced them
to make an excursion to Smyrna. There, on the 28th of
March, the second canto of *Childe Harold*, begun in the
previous autumn at Janina, was completed. They remained in the neighbourhood, visiting Ephesus, without
poetical result further than a reference to the jackals, in
the *Siege of Corinth;* and on April 11th left by the
"Salsette," a frigate on its way to Constantinople. The
vessel touched at the Troad, and Byron spent some time
on land, snipe-shooting, and rambling among the reputed
ruins of Ilium. The poet characteristically, in *Don Juan*

and elsewhere, attacks the sceptics, and then half ridi-
cules the belief.

> I've stood upon Achilles' tomb,
> And heard Troy doubted! Time will doubt of Rome!
>     \*      \*      \*      \*      \*
> There, on the green and village-cotted hill, is,
> Flank'd by the Hellespont, and by the sea,
> Entomb'd the bravest of the brave Achilles.—
> They say so : Bryant says the contrary.

Being again detained in the Dardanelles, waiting for a
fair wind, Byron landed on the European side, and swam,
in company with Lieutenant Ekenhead, from Sestos to
Abydos—a performance of which he boasts some twenty
times. The strength of the current is the main difficulty
of a feat, since so surpassed as to have passed from notice ;
but it was a tempting theme for classical allusions. At
length, on May 14, he reached Constantinople, exalted
the Golden Horn above all the sights he had seen, and
now first abandoned his design of travelling to Persia.
Galt, and other more or less gossipping travellers, have
accumulated a number of incidents of the poet's life at
this period, of his fanciful dress, blazing in scarlet and
gold, and of his sometimes absurd contentions for the
privileges of rank—as when he demanded precedence of
the English ambassador in an interview with the Sultan,
and, on its refusal, could only be pacified by the assur-
ances of the Austrian internuncio. In converse with
indifferent persons he displayed a curious alternation of
frankness and hauteur, and indulged a habit of letting
people up and down, by which he frequently gave offence.
More interesting are narratives of the suggestion of some
of his verses, as the slave-market in *Don Juan,* and the
spectacle of the dead criminal tossed on the waves, revived

in the *Bride of Abydos*. One example is, if we except Dante's *Ugolino*, the most remarkable instance in literature of the expansion, without the weakening, of the horrible. Take first Mr. Hobhouse's plain prose : " The sensations produced by the state of the weather"—it was wretched and stormy when they left the " Salsette" for the city—"and leaving a comfortable cabin, were in unison with the impressions which we felt when, passing under the palace of the Sultans, and gazing at the gloomy cypress which rises above the walls, we saw two dogs gnawing a dead body." After this we may measure the almost fiendish force of a morbid imagination brooding over the incident,—

And he saw the lean dogs beneath the wall
Hold o'er the dead their carnival :
Gorging and growling o'er carcass and limb,
They were too busy to bark at him.
From a Tartar's skull they had stripp'd the flesh,
As ye peel the fig when its fruit is fresh ;
And their white tusks crunch'd on the whiter skull,
As it slipp'd through their jaws when their edge grew dull.

No one ever more persistently converted the incidents of travel into poetic material ; but sometimes in doing so he borrowed more largely from his imagination than his memory, as in the description of the seraglio, of which there is reason to doubt his having seen more than the entrance.

Byron and Hobhouse set sail from Constantinople on the 14th July, 1810—the latter to return direct to England, a determination which, from no apparent fault on either side, the former did not regret. One incident of the passage derives interest from its possible consequence. Taking up, and unsheathing, a yataghan which he found

on the quarter deck, he remarked, " I should like to know
how a person feels after committing a murder." This
harmless piece of melodrama—the idea of which is
expanded in Mr. Dobell's *Balder* and parodied in
*Firmilian*—may have been the basis of a report afterwards circulated, and accepted among others by Goethe,
that his lordship had committed a murder; hence,
obviously, the character of *Lara*, and the mystery of
*Manfred!* The poet parted from his friend at Zea
(Ceos): after spending some time in solitude on the little
island, he returned to Athens, and there renewed acquaintance with his school friend, the Marquis of Sligo, who
after a few days accompanied him to Corinth. They
then separated, and Byron went on to Patras in the
Morea, where he had business with the Consul. He
dates from there at the close of July. It is impossible
to give a consecutive account of his life during the next
ten months, a period consequently filled up with the
contradictory and absurd mass of legends before referred
to. A few facts only of any interest are extricable.
During at least half of the time his head-quarters were at
Athens, where he again met his friend the Marquis,
associated with the English Consul and Lady Hester
Stanhope, studied Romaic in a Franciscan monastery—
where he saw and conversed with a motley crew of French,
Italians, Danes, Greeks, Turks, and Americans,—wrote to
his mother and others, saying he had swum from Sestos
to Abydos, was sick of Fletcher bawling for beef and
beer, had done with authorship, and hoped on his return
to lead a quiet recluse life. He nevertheless made notes
to *Harold*, composed the *Hints from Horace* and the
*Curse of Minerva*, and presumably brooded over, and
outlined in his mind, many of his verse romances. We

F

hear no more of the *Maid of Athens*, but there is no
fair ground to doubt that the *Giaour* was suggested
by his rescue of a young woman whom, for the fault
of an amour with some Frank, a party of Janissaries
were about to throw, sewn up in a sack, into the sea.
Mr. Galt gives no authority for his statement, that the
girl's deliverer was the original cause of her sentence. We
may rest assured that if it had been so, Byron himself
would have told us of it.

A note to the *Siege of Corinth* is suggestive of his
unequalled restlessness. "I visited all three—Tripolitza,
Napoli, and Argos—in 1810-11 ; and in the course of
journeying through the country, from my first arrival in
1809, crossed the Isthmus eight times on my way from
Attica to the Morea. In the latter locality we find
him during the autumn the honoured guest of the Vizier
Valhi (a son of Ali Pasha), who presented him with a
fine horse. During a second visit to Patras, in September,
he was attacked by the same sort of marsh fever from
which, fourteen years afterwards, in the near neighbourhood, he died. On his recovery, in October, he complains
of having been nearly killed by the heroic measures of
the native doctors : "One of them trusts to his genius,
never having studied ; the other, to a campaign of eighteen
months *against* the sick of Otranto, which he made in his
youth with great effect. When I was seized with my disorder,
I protested against both these assassins, but in vain." He
was saved by the zeal of his servants, who asseverated that
if his lordship died they would take good care the doctors
should also ; on which the learned men discontinued their
visits, and the patient revived. On his final return to
Athens, the restoration of his health was retarded by one
of his long courses of reducing diet ; he lived mainly on

rice, and vinegar and water. From that city he writes in
the early spring, intimating his intention of proceeding to
Egypt; but Mr. Hanson, his man of business, ceasing to
send him remittances, the scheme was abandoned. Beset
by letters about his debts, he again declares his determination to hold fast by Newstead, adding that if the
place which is his only tie to England is sold, he won't
come back at all. Life on the shores of the Archipelago
is far cheaper and happier, and "Ubi bene ibi patria," for
such a citizen of the world as he has become. Later he
went to Malta, and was detained there by another bad
attack of tertian fever. The next record of consequence is
from the "Volage" frigate, at sea, June 29, 1811, when he
writes in a despondent strain to Hodgson, that he is returning home "without a hope, and almost without a desire,"
to wrangle with creditors and lawyers about executions and
coal pits. "In short, I am sick and sorry; and when I have
a little repaired my irreparable affairs, away I shall march,
either to campaign in Spain, or back again to the East, where
I can at least have cloudless skies and a cessation from im-
pertinence. I am sick of fops, and poesy, and prate, and
shall leave the whole Castalian state to Bufo, or anybody
else. Howbeit, I have written some 4000 lines, of one
kind or another, on my travels." With these, and a collection of marbles, and skulls, and hemlock, and tortoises,
and servants, he reached London about the middle of July,
and remained there, making some arrangements about
business and publication. On the 23rd we have a short
but kind letter to his mother, promising to pay her a visit
on his way to Rochdale. "You know you are a vixen, but
keep some champagne for me," he had written from
abroad. On receipt of the letter she remarked, "If I
should be dead before he comes down, what a strange

thing it would be." Towards the close of the month she
had an attack so alarming that he was summoned ; but
before he had time to arrive she had expired, on the 1st
of August, in a fit of rage brought on by reading an
upholsterer's bill. On the way Byron heard the intelli-
gence, and wrote to Dr. Pigot : " I now feel the truth of
Mrs. Gray's observation, that we can only have *one*
mother. Peace be with her ! " On arriving at Newstead,
all their storms forgotten, the son was so affected that he
did not trust himself to go to the funeral, but stood
dreamily gazing at the cortége from the gate of the Abbey.
Five days later, Charles S. Matthews was drowned.

# CHAPTER V.

THE deaths of Long, Wingfield, Eddlestone, Matthews, and of his mother, had narrowed the circle of the poet's early companions; and, though he talks of each loss in succession as if it had been that of an only friend, we can credit a degree of loneliness, and excuse a certain amount of bitterness in the feelings with which he returned to London. He had at this time seen very little of the only relative whom he ever deeply loved. He and his half-sister met casually in 1804, and again in the following year. After her marriage (1807), Byron writes from abroad (1810), regretting having distressed her by his quarrel with Lord Carlisle. In 1811 she is mentioned as reversionary heiress of his estate. Towards the close of 1813, there are two allusions which testify to their mutual affection. Next we come to the interesting series of letters of 1815-16, published with the Memoir of Mr. Hodgson, to whom, along with Hobhouse and Scrope Davies, his lordship in a will and codicil leaves the management of his property. Harness appears frequently at this period among his surviving intimates: to this list there was shortly added another. In speaking of his *Bards and Reviewers*, the author makes occa-

sional reference to the possibility of his being called to
account for some of his attacks. His expectation was
realized by a letter from the poet Moore, dated Dublin,
Jan. 1, 1810, couched in peremptory terms, demanding
to know if his lordship avowed the authorship of the
insults contained in the poem. This letter, being entrusted to Mr. Hodgson, was not forwarded to Byron
abroad ; but shortly after his return, he received another
in more conciliatory terms, renewing the complaint. To
this he replied in a stiff but manly letter, that he had
never meant to insult Mr. Moore ; but that he was, if
necessary, ready to give him satisfaction. Moore accepting the explanation, somewhat querulously complained of
his advances to friendship not being received. Byron
again replied that much as he would feel honoured by
Mr. Moore's acquaintance, he being practically threatened
by the irate Irishman could hardly make the first advances.
This called forth a sort of apology ; the correspondents
met at the house of Mr. Rogers, and out of the somewhat
awkward circumstances, owing to the frankness of the
" noble author," as the other ever after delights to call
him, arose the life-long intimacy which had such various
and lasting results. Moore has been called a false friend
to Byron, and a traitor to his memory. The judgment
is somewhat harsh, but the association between them was
unfortunate. Thomas Moore had some sterling qualities.
His best satirical pieces are inspired by a real indignation,
and lit up by a genuine humour. He was also an exquisite musician in words, and must have been occasionally
a fascinating companion. But he was essentially a
worldling, and, as such, a superficial critic. He encouraged the shallow affectations of his great friend's
weaker work, and recoiled in alarm before the daring

defiance of his stronger. His criticisms on all Byron
wrote and felt seriously on religion are almost worthy of
a conventicle. His letters to others on *Manfred*, and *Cain*,
and *Don Juan*, are the expression of sentiments which
he had never the courage to state explicitly to the author.
On the other hand, Byron was attracted beyond reasonable measure by his gracefully deferential manners, paid
too much regard to his opinions, and overestimated his
genius. For the subsequent destruction of the memoirs,
urged by Mr. Hobhouse and Mrs. Leigh, he was not
wholly responsible ; though a braver man, having accepted
the position of his lordship's literary legatee, with the
express understanding that he would see to the fulfilment
of the wishes of his dead friend, would have to the
utmost resisted their total frustration.

Meanwhile, on landing in England, the poet had placed
in the hands of Mr. Dallas the *Hints from Horace*,
which he intended to have brought out by the publisher
Cawthorne. Of this performance—an inferior edition,
relieved by a few strong touches, of the *Bards and
Reviewers*—Dallas ventured to express his disapproval.
" Have you no other result of your travels ?" he asked ;
and got for answer, " A few short pieces ; and a lot
of Spenserian stanzas ; not worth troubling you with,
but you are welcome to them." Dallas took the remark literally, saw they were a safe success, and
assumed to himself the merit of the discovery, the risks,
and the profits. It is the converse of the story of
Gabriel Harvey and the *Faery Queene.* The first two
cantos of *Childe Harold* bear no comparison with the
legend of *Una and the Red Cross Knight;* but there
was no mistake about their proof of power, their novelty,
and adaptation to a public taste as yet unjaded by elo-

quent and imaginative descriptions of foreign scenery, manners, and climates.

The poem—after being submitted to Gifford, in defiance of the protestations of the author, who feared that the reference might seem to seek the favour of the august *Quarterly*—was accepted by Mr. Murray, and proceeded through the press, subject to change and additions, during the next five months. The *Hints from Horace*, fortunately postponed and then suspended, appeared posthumously in 1831. Byron remained at Newstead till the close of October, negotiating with creditors and lawyers, and engaged in a correspondence about his publications, in the course of which he deprecates any identification of himself and his hero, though he had at first called him Childe Byron. "Instruct Mr. Murray," he entreats, "not to call the work 'Child of Harrow's Pilgrimage,' as he has done to some of my astonished friends, who wrote to inquire after my *sanity*, as well they might." At the end of the month we find him in London, again indulging in a voyage in "the ship of fools," in which Moore claims to have accompanied him; but at the same time exhibiting remarkable shrewdness in reference to the affairs of his household. In February, 1812, he again declares to Hodgson his resolve to leave England for ever, and fix himself in "one of the fairest islands of the East." On the 27th he made in the House of Lords his speech on a Bill to introduce special penalties against the frame-breakers of Nottingham. This effort, on which he received many compliments, led among other results to a friendly correspondence with Lord Holland. On April 21st of the same year, he again addressed the House on behalf of Roman Catholic Emancipation; and in June, 1813, in favour of Major Cartwright's petition.

On all these occasions, as afterwards on the continent, Byron espoused the Liberal side of politics. But his rôle was that of Manlius or Cæsar, and he never fails to remind us that he himself was *for* the people, not *of* them. His latter speeches, owing partly to his delivery, blamed as too Asiatic, were less successful. To a reader the three seem much on the same level. They are clever, but evidently set performances, and leave us no ground to suppose that the poet's abandonment of a parliamentary career was a serious loss to the nation.

On the 29th of February the first and second cantos of *Childe Harold* appeared. An early copy was sent to Mrs. Leigh, with the inscription: "To Augusta, my dearest sister and my best friend, who has ever loved me much better than I deserved, this volume is presented by her father's son and most affectionate brother, B." The book ran through seven editions in four weeks. The effect of the first edition of Burns, and the sale of Scott's *Lays*, are the only parallels in modern poetic literature to this success. All eyes were suddenly fastened on the author, who let his satire sleep, and threw politics aside, to be the romancer of his day and for two years the darling of society. Previous to the publition, Mr. Moore confesses to have gratified his lordship with the expression of the fear that *Childe Harold* was too good for the age. Its success was due to the reverse being the truth. It was just on the level of its age. Its flowing verse, defaced by rhymical faults perceptible only to finer ears, its prevailing sentiment, occasional boldness relieved by pleasing platitudes, its half affected rakishness, here and there elevated by a rush as of morning air, and its frequent richness—not yet, as afterwards, splendour—of description, were all appreciated by the

fashionable London of the Regency; while the comparatively mild satire, not keen enough to scarify, only gave a
more piquant flavour to the whole. Byron's genius, yet in
the green leaf, was not too far above the clever masses of
pleasure-loving manhood by which it was surrounded. It
was natural that the address on the reopening of Drury
Lane theatre should be written by " the world's new joy"—
the first great English poet-peer; as natural as that in his
only published satire of the period he should inveigh
against almost the only amusement in which he could
not share. The address was written at the request of
Lord Holland, when of some hundred competitive pieces
none had been found exactly suitable—a circumstance
which gave rise to the famous parodies entitled *The
Rejected Addresses*—and it was thought that the ultimate
choice would conciliate all rivalry. The care which
Byron bestowed on the correction of the first draft of
this piece, is characteristic of his habit of writing off his
poems at a gush, and afterwards carefully elaborating
them.

*The Waltz* was published anonymously in April, 1813.
It was followed in May by the *Giaour*, the first of the
flood of verse romances which, during the three succeeding years, he poured forth with impetuous fluency, and
which were received with almost unrestrained applause.
The plots and sentiments and imagery are similar in them
all. The Giaour steals the mistress of Hassan, who
revenges his honour by drowning her. The Giaour
escapes; returns, kills Hassan, and then goes to a
monastery. In the *Bride of Abydos*, published in the
December of the same year, Giaffir wants to marry his
daughter Zuleika to Carasman Pasha. She runs off with
Selim, her reputed brother—in reality her cousin, and so

at last her legitimate lover. They are caught ; he is slain
in fight; she dies, to slow music. In the *Corsair*, published January, 1814, Conrad, a pirate, and man of " one
virtue and a thousand crimes ! " is beloved by Medora, who
on his predatory expeditions, sits waiting for him (like
Hassan's and Sisera's mother) in a tower. On one of
these he attacks Seyd Pasha, and is overborne by superior
force ; but Gulnare, a female slave of Seyd, kills her
master, and runs off with Conrad, who finds Medora dead
and vanishes. In *Lara*, the sequel to this—written in
May and June, published in August—a man of mystery
appears in the Morea, with a page, Kaled. After adventures worthy of Mrs. Radcliffe—from whose Schledoni the
Giaour is said to have been drawn—Lara falls in battle
with his deadly foe, Ezzelin, and turns out to be Conrad,
while Kaled is of course Gulnare. The *Hebrew Melodies*,
written in December, 1814, are interesting, in connexion
with the author's early familiarity with the Old Testa-
ment, and from the force and music that mark the best of
them ; but they can hardly be considered an important
contribution to the devotional verse of England. The
*Siege of Corinth* and *Parisina*, composed after his
marriage in the summer and autumn of 1815, appeared in
the following year. The former is founded on the siege
of the city, when the Turks took it from Menotti ; but our
attention is concentrated on Alp the renegade, another
sketch from the same protoplastic ruffian, who leads on
the Turks, is in love with the daughter of the governor
of the city, tries to save her, but dies. The poem is
frequently vigorous, but it ends badly. *Parisina*, though
unequal, is on the whole a poem of a higher order than
the others of the period. The trial scene exhibits some
dramatic power, and the shriek of the lady mingling

with Ugo's funeral dirge lingers in our ears, along with
the convent bells—

> In the grey square turret swinging,
> With a deep sound, to and fro,
> Heavily to the heart they go.

These romances belong to the same period of the author's
poetic career as the first two cantos of *Childe Harold.*
They followed one another like brilliant fireworks.   They
all exhibit a command of words, a sense of melody, and a
flow of rhythm and rhyme, which mastered Moore and
even Scott on their own ground.   None of them are
wanting in passages, as " He that hath bent him o'er the
dead," and the description of Alp leaning against a column,
which strike deeper than any verse of either of these
writers.   But there is an air of melodrama in them
all.   Harmonious delights of novel readers, they will
not stand against the winnowing wind of deliberate
criticism.   They harp on the same string, without the
variations of a Paganini.   They are potentially endless
reproductions of one phase of an ill-regulated mind—the
picture of the same quasi-melancholy vengeful man, who
knows no friend but a dog, and reads on the tombs of the
great only " the  glory and the nothing of a name," the
exile who cannot flee from himself, " the wandering out-
law of his own dark  mind," who has not loved the world
nor the world him,—

> Whose heart was form'd for softness, warp'd by wrong,
> Betray'd too early, and beguiled too long—

all this, *decies repetita,* grows into a weariness and
vexation.   Mr. Carlyle harshly compares it to the screaming of a meat-jack.   The reviewers and the public of the

time thought differently. Jeffrey, penitent for the early
*faux pas* of his *Review*, as Byron remained penitent for his
answering assault, writes of *Lara*, "Passages of it may be
put into competition with anything that poetry has produced in point either of pathos or energy." Moore—who
afterwards wrote, not to Byron, that seven devils had
entered into *Manfred*—professes himself "enraptured
with it." Fourteen thousand copies of the *Corsair*
were sold in a day. But hear the author's own half-
boast, half-apology : "*Lara* I wrote while undressing after
coming home from balls and masquerades, in the year of
revelry 1814. The *Bride* was written in four, the
*Corsair* in ten days. This I take to be a humiliating confession, as it proves my own want of judgment in publishing, and the public's in reading, things which cannot have
stamina for permanence."

The pecuniary profits accruing to Byron from his works
began with *Lara*, for which he received 700*l*. He had
made over to Mr. Dallas, besides other gifts to the
same ungrateful recipient, the profits of *Harold*, amounting to 600*l*., and of the *Corsair*, which brought 525*l*.
The proceeds of the *Giaour* and the *Bride* were also
surrendered.

During this period, 1813—1816, he had become familiar
with all the phases of London society, "tasted their
pleasures," and, towards the close, "felt their decay."
His associates in those years were of two classes—men
of the world, and authors. Fêted and courted in all
quarters, he patronized the theatres, became in 1815
a member of the Drury Lane Committee, "liked the
dandies," including Beau Brummell, and was introduced
to the Regent. Their interview, in June 1812, in the
course of which the latter paid unrestrained compli-

ments to *Harold* and the poetry of Scott, is naively
referred to by Mr. Moore " as reflecting even still more
honour on the Sovereign himself than on the two poets."
Byron, in a different spirit, writes to Lord Holland : " I
have now great hope, in the event of Mr. Pye's decease,
of warbling truth at Court, like Mr. Mallet of indifferent
memory. Consider, one hundred marks a year ! besides
the wine and the disgrace." We can hardly conceive the
future author of the *Vision of Judgment* writing odes
to dictation. He does not seem to have been much
fascinated with the first gentleman of Europe, whom at no
distant date he assailed in the terrible " Avatar," and left -
the laureateship to Mr. Southey.

About this time a communication from Mr Murray in
Among leaders in art and letters he was brought into
more or less intimate contact with Sir Humphry Davy, the
Edgeworths, Sir James Mackintosh, Colman the dramatic
author, the elder Kean, Monk Lewis, Grattan, Curran,
and Madame de Staël. Of a meeting of the last two he
remarks, " It was like the confluence of the Rhone and
the Sâone, and they were both so ugly that I could
not help wondering how the best intellects of France
and Ireland could have taken up respectively such
residences."

About this time a communication from Mr Murray in
reference to the meeting with the Regent led to a letter
from Sir Walter Scott to Lord Byron, the beginning of a
life-long friendship, and one of the most pleasing pages
of biography. These two great men were for a season
perpetually pitted against one another, as the foremost
competitors for literary favour. When *Rokeby* came out,
contemporaneously with the *Giaour*, the undergraduates of
Oxford and Cambridge ran races to catch the first copies, and
laid bets as to which of the rivals would win. During the

anti-Byronic fever of 1840—1860 they were perpetually
contrasted as the representatives of the manly and the
morbid schools.  A later sentimentalism has affected to
despise the work of both.  The fact therefore that from
an early period the men themselves knew each other as
they were, is worth illustrating.

Scott's letter, in which a generous recognition of the
pleasure he had derived from the work of the English
poet, was followed by a manly remonstrance on the subject of the attack in the *Bards and Reviewers*, drew from
Byron in the following month (July 1812) an answer
in the same strain, descanting on the Prince's praises of
the *Lay* and *Marmion*, and candidly apologizing for the
" evil works of his nonage."   " The satire," he remarks,
" was written when I was very young and very angry, and
fully bent on displaying my wrath and my wit ; and now
I am haunted by the ghosts of my wholesale assertions."
This, in turn, called forth another letter to Byron eager
for more of his verses, with a cordial invitation to Abbots-
ford on the ground of Scotland's maternal claim on
him, and asking for information about Pegasus and
Parnassus.  After this the correspondence continues with
greater freedom, and the same display on either side of
mutual respect.   When Scott says " the *Giaour* is praised
among our mountains," and Byron returns " *Waverley* is
the best novel I have read," there is no suspicion of
flattery—it is the interchange of compliments between
men,

Et cantare pares et respondere parati.

They talk in just the same manner to third parties.   " I
gave over writing romances," says the elder, in the spirit of
a great-hearted gentleman, " because Byron beat me.  He

hits the mark, where I don't even pretend to fledge my
arrow.  He has access to a stream of sentiment unknown to
me."  The younger, on the other hand, deprecates the com-
parisons that were being invidiously drawn between them.
He presents his copy of the *Giaour* to Scott, with the
phrase " To the monarch of Parnassus," and compares the
feeling of those who cavilled at his fame to that of the
Athenians towards Aristides.  From those sentiments,
he never swerves, recognizing to the last the breadth
of character of the most generous of his critics, and
referring to him, during his later years in Italy, as the
Wizard and the Ariosto of the North.  A meeting was at
length arranged between them.  Scott looked forward to
it with anxious interest, humorously remarking that Byron
should say,—

Art thou the man whom men famed Grissell call?

And he reply—

Art thou the still more famed Tom Thumb the small?

They met in London during the spring of 1815.  The
following sentences are from Sir Walter's account of it :
—" Report had prepared me to meet a man of peculiar
habits and quick temper, and I had some doubts
whether we were likely to suit each other in society.  I
was most agreeably disappointed in this respect.  I found
Lord Byron in the highest degree courteous, and even kind.
We met for an hour or two almost daily in Mr. Murray's
drawing-room, and found a great deal to say to each other.
Our sentiments agreed a good deal, except upon the subjects of religion and politics, upon neither of which I was
inclined to believe that Lord Byron entertained very fixed
opinions.  On politics he used sometimes to express a high

strain of what is now called Liberalism ; but it appeared
to me that the pleasure it afforded him as a vehicle of
displaying his wit and satire against individuals in office
was at the bottom of this habit of thinking.  At heart, I
would have termed Byron a patrician on principle.  His
reading did not seem to me to have been very extensive.
I remember repeating to him the fine poem of Hardyknute,
and some one asked me what I could possibly have been
telling Byron by which he was so much agitated.  I saw
him for the last time in (September) 1815, after I
returned from France ; he dined or lunched with me at
Long's in Bond Street.  I never saw him so full of
gaiety and good humour.  The day of this interview was
the most interesting I ever spent.  Several letters passed between us—one perhaps every half year.  Like the old heroes
in Homer we exchanged gifts ; I gave Byron a beautiful
dagger mounted with gold, which had been the property
of the redoubted Elfi Bey.  But I was to play the part
of Diomed in the *Iliad*, for Byron sent me, some time
after, a large sepulchral vase of silver, full of dead men's
bones, found within the land walls of Athens.  He was
often melancholy, almost gloomy.  When I observed him
in this humour I used either to wait till it went off of its
own accord, or till some natural and easy mode occurred
of leading him into conversation, when the shadows almost
always left his countenance, like the mist arising from a
landscape.  I think I also remarked in his temper starts
of suspicion, when he seemed to pause and consider
whether there had not been a secret and perhaps offensive
meaning in something that was said to him.  In this case
I also judged it best to let his mind, like a troubled spring,
work itself clear, which it did in a minute or two.  A
downright steadiness of manner was the way to his good

opinion. Will Rose, looking by accident at his feet, saw him scowling furiously; but on his showing no conscious- ness, his lordship resumed his easy manner. What I liked about him, besides his boundless genius, was his generosity of spirit as well as of purse, and his utter contempt of all the affectations of literature. He liked Moore and me because, with all our other differ- ences, we were both good-natured fellows, not caring to maintain our dignity, enjoying the *mot-pour-rire*. He wrote from impulse never from effort, and therefore I have always reckoned Burns and Byron the most genuine poetic geniuses of my time, and of half a century before me. We have many men of high poetic talents, but none of that ever-gushing and perennial fountain of natural waters."

Scott, like all hale men of sound sense, regretted the almost fatal incontinence which, in the year of his greatest private troubles, led his friend to make a parade of them before the public. He speaks more than once of his unhappy tendency to exhibit himself as the dying gladiator, and even compares him to his peacock, screech- ing before his window because he chooses to bivouack apart from his mate ; but he read a copy of the Ravenna diary without altering his view that his lordship was his own worst maligner. Scott, says Lockhart, considered Byron the only poet of transcendent talents we had had since Dryden. There is preserved a curious record of his meeting with a greater poet than Dryden, but one whose greatness neither he nor Scott suspected. Mr. Crabbe Robinson reports Wordsworth to have said, in Charles Lamb's chambers, about the year 1808, "These reviewers put me out of patience. Here is a young man who has written a volume of poetry ; and these fellows, just because he is a lord, set upon him. The young man will do something, if he goes on as he has begun. But these reviewers seem to think that nobody may write poetry unless he lives in a garret." Years after, Lady Byron, on being told this, exclaimed, "Ah, if Byron had known that, he would never have attacked Wordsworth. He went one day to meet him at dinner, and I said, ' Well, how did the young poet get on with the old one ?' ' Why, to tell the truth,' said he, ' I had but one feeling from the beginning of the visit to the end, and that was *reverence.*' " Similarly, he began by being on good terms with Southey, and after a meeting at Holland House, wrote enthusiastically of his prepossessing appearance.

Byron and the leaders of the so-called Lake School were, at starting, common heirs of the revolutionary spirit ; they were, either in their social views or personal feelings, to a large extent influenced by the most morbid, though in some respects the most magnetic, genius of modern France, J. J. Rousseau ; but their temperaments were in many respects fundamentally diverse ; and the pre-established discord between them ere long began to make itself manifest in their following out widely divergent paths. Wordsworth's return to nature had been preluded by Cowper ; that of Byron by Burns. The revival of the one ripened into a restoration of simpler manners and old beliefs ; the other was the spirit of the storm. When they had both become recognized powers, neither appreciated the work of the other. A few years after this date Byron wrote of Wordsworth, to a common admirer of both : "I take leave to differ from you as freely as I once agreed with you. His performances, since the *Lyrical Ballads,* are miserably inadequate to the ability that lurks within him. There is, undoubtedly, much natural talent spilt over the *Excursion* ; but it is rain upon rocks, where it stands and stagnates ; or rain upon sand, where it falls without fertilizing." This criticism with others in like strain, was addressed to Mr. Leigh Hunt, to whom, in 1812, when enduring for radicalism's sake a very comfortable incarceration, Byron had, in company with Moore, paid a courteous visit.

Of the correspondence of this period—flippant, trenchant, or sparkling—few portions are more calculated to excite a smile than the record of his frequent resolutions made, reasseverated, and broken, to have done with literature ; even going the length on some occasions of threatening to suppress his works, and, if possible, recall the existing copies. He affected being a man of the world unmercifully, and had a real delight in clever companions who assumed the same rôle. Frequent allusion is made to his intercourse with Erskine and Sheridan : the latter he is never tired of praising, as "the author of the best modern comedy (*School for Scandal*), the best farce (*The Critic*), and the best oration (the famous Begum speech) ever heard in this country." They spent many an evening together, and probably cracked many a bottle. It is Byron who tells the story of Sheridan being found in a gutter in a sadly incapable state ; and, on some one asking "Who is this ?" stammering out "Wilberforce." On one occasion he speaks of coming out of a tavern with the dramatist, when they both found the staircase in a very cork-screw condition : and elsewhere, of encountering a Mr. C——, who "had no notion of meeting with a bon-vivant in a scribbler," and summed the poet's eulogy with the phrase, "he drinks like a man." Hunt, the tattler, who observed his lordship's habits in

Italy, with the microscope of malice ensconced within the same walls, makes it a charge against his host that he would not drink like a man. Once for all it may be noted, that although there was no kind of excess in which Byron, whether from bravado or inclination, failed occasionally to indulge, he was never for any stretch of time given over, like Burns, to what is technically termed intemperance. His head does not seem to have been strong, and under the influence of stimulants he may have been led to talk a great deal of his dangerous nonsense. But though he could not say, with Wordsworth, that only once, at Cambridge, had his brain been "excited by the fumes of wine," his prevailing sins were in other directions.

# CHAPTER VI

"As for poets," says Scott, "I have seen all the best of my time and country, and, though Burns had the most glorious eye imaginable, I never thought any of them would come up to an artist's notion of the character, except Byron. His countenance is a thing to dream of." Coleridge writes to the same effect, in language even stronger. We have from all sides similar testimony to the personal beauty which led the unhappiest of his devotees to exclaim, "That pale face is my fate !"

Southern critics, as De Chasles, Castelar, even Mazzini, have dealt leniently with the poet's relations to the other sex ; and Elze extends to him in this regard the same excessive stretch of charity. "Dear Childe Harold," exclaims the German professor, "was positively besieged by women. They have, in truth, no right to complain of him : from his childhood he had seen them on their worst side." It is the casuistry of hero-worship to deny that Byron was unjust to women, not merely in isolated instances, but in his prevailing views of their character and claims. "I regard them," he says, in a passage only distinguished from others by more extravagant petulance, "as very pretty but inferior creatures, who are as little in their place at our tables as they would be in our council

chambers. The whole of the present system with regard
to the female sex is a remnant of the barbarism of the
chivalry of our forefathers. I look on them as grown-up
children ; but, like a foolish mamma, I am constantly the
slave of one of them. The Turks shut up their women,
and are much happier ; give a woman a looking-glass and
burnt almonds, and she will be content."

In contrast with this, we have the moods in which he
drew his pictures of Angiolina, and Haidee, and Aurora
Raby, and wrote the invocations to the shade of Astarte,
and his letters in prose and verse to Augusta ; but the
above passage could never have been written by Chaucer,
or Spenser, or Shakespeare, or Shelley. The class whom
he was reviling seemed, however, during " the day of his
destiny," bent on confirming his judgment by the blindness of their worship. His rank and fame, the glittering
splendour of his verse, the romance of his travels, his
picturesque melancholy and affectation of mysterious
secrets, combined with the magic of his presence to
bewitch and bewilder them. The dissenting malcontents,
condemned as prudes and blues, had their revenge.
Generally, we may say that women who had not written
books adored Byron ; women who had written or were
writing books distrusted, disliked, and made him a moral
to adorn their tales, often to point their fables with. He
was by the one set caressed and spoilt, and "beguiled too
long ;" by the other, "betrayed too late." The recent
memoirs of Frances Ann Kemble present a curious record
of the process of passing from one extreme to the other.
She dwells on the fascination exerted over her mind
by the first reading of his poetry, and tells how she
" fastened on the book with a grip like steel," and carried
it off and hid it under her pillow ; how it affected her

"like an evil potion," and stirred her whole being with a
tempest of excitement, till finally she, with equal weakness, flung it aside, "resolved to read that grand poetry
no more, and broke through the thraldom of that powerful
spell." The confession brings before us a type of the
transitions of the century, on its way from the Byronic to
the anti-Byronic fever, of which later state Mrs. Jamie-
son, Mrs. Norton, and Miss Martineau are among the
most pronounced representatives.

Byron's garrulity with regard to those delicate matters
on which men of more prudence or chivalry are wont to
set the seal of silence, has often the same practical effect as
reticence ; for he talks so much at large—every page of his
Journal being, by his own admission, apt to " confute and
abjure its predecessor "—that we are often none the wiser.
Amid a mass of conjecture, it is manifest that during the
years between his return from Greece and final expa-
triation (1811—1816), including the whole period of his
social glory—though not yet of his solid fame—he was
lured into liaisons of all sorts and shades. Some, now
acknowledged as innocent, were blared abroad by tongues
less skilled in pure invention than in distorting truth. On
others, as commonplaces of a temperament " all meridian,"
it were waste of time to dwell. Byron rarely put aside
a pleasure in his path ; but his passions were seldom un-
accompanied by affectionate emotions, genuine while they
lasted. The verses to the memory of a lost love veiled as
"Thyrza," of moderate artistic merit, were not, as Moore
alleges, mere plays of imagination, but records of a sincere
grief.[1] Another intimacy exerted so much influence on this

[1] Mr. Trelawny says that Thyrza was a cousin, but that on
this subject Byron was always reticent. Mr. Minto, as we have
seen, associates her with the disguised girl of 1807-8.

VI.] MARRIAGE, AND FAREWELL TO ENGLAND. 89

phase of the poet's career, that to pass it over would be like
omitting Vanessa's name from the record of Swift. Lady
Caroline Lamb, granddaughter of the first Earl Spencer, was
one of those few women of our climate who, by their romantic impetuosity, recall the " children of the sun." She read
Burns in her ninth year, and in her thirteenth idealized
William Lamb (afterwards Lord Melbourne) as a statue of
Liberty. In her nineteenth (1805) she married him, and
lived for some years, during which she was a reigning
belle and toast, a domestic life only marred by occasional eccentricities. Rogers, whom in a letter to
Lady Morgan she numbers among her lovers, said she
ought to know the new poet, who was three years
her junior, and the introduction took place in March,
1812. After the meeting, she wrote in her journal,
"Mad—bad—and dangerous to know;" but, when the
fashionable Apollo called at Melbourne House, she " flew
to beautify herself." Flushed by his conquest, he spent a
great part of the following year in her company, during
which time the apathy or self-confidence of the husband
laughed at the worship of the hero. " Conrad " detailed
his travels and adventures, interested her, by his woes,
dictated her amusements, invited her guests, and seems
to have set rules to the establishment. " Medora,"
on the other hand, made no secret of her devotion, declared that they were affinities, and offered
him her jewels. But after the first excitement, he began
to grow weary of her talk about herself, and could not
praise her indifferent verses : " he grew moody, and she
fretful, when their mutual egotisms jarred." Byron at
length concurred in her being removed for a season to her
father's house in Ireland, on which occasion he wrote one
of his glowing farewell letters. When she came back,

matters were little better. The would-be Juliet beset the
poet with renewed advances, on one occasion penetrating
to his rooms in the disguise of a page, on another threatening to stab herself with a pair of scissors, and again,
developing into a Medea, offering her gratitude to any
one who would kill him. "The 'Agnus' is furious," he
writes to Hodgson, in February, 1813, in one of the somewhat ungenerous bursts to which he was too easily provoked. "You can have no idea of the horrible and
absurd things she has said and done since (really from
the best motives) I withdrew my homage. . . . . The
business of last summer I broke off, and now the amusement of the gentle fair is writing letters literally threatening my life." With one member of the family, Lady
Melbourne, Mr. Lamb's mother, and sister of Sir Ralph
Milbanke, he remained throughout on terms of pleasant
intimacy. He appreciated the talent and sense, and was
ready to profit by the experience and tact of " the cleverest
of women." But her well-meant advice had unfortunate
results, for it was on her suggestion that he became a
suitor for the hand of her niece, Miss Milbanke. Byron
first proposed to this lady in 1813 ; his offer was refused,
but so graciously that they continued to correspond on
friendly, which gradually grew into intimate terms, and
his second offer, towards the close of the following year,
was accepted.

After a series of vain protests, and petulant warnings
against her cousin by marriage, who she said was
punctual at church, and learned, and knew statistics, but
was "not for Conrad, no, no, no !" Lady Caroline
lapsed into an attitude of fixed hostility ; and shortly
after the crash came, and her predictions were realized,
vented her wrath in the now almost forgotten novel of

*Glenarvon*, in which some of Byron's real features were represented in conjunction with many fantastic additions. Madame de Staël was kind enough to bring a copy of the book before his notice when they met on the Lake of Geneva, but he seems to have been less moved by it than by most attacks. We must however, bear in mind his own admission in a parallel case. "I say I am perfectly calm; I am, nevertheless, in a fury." Over the sad vista of the remaining years of the unhappy lady's life we need not linger. During a considerable part of it she appears hovering about the thin line that separates some kinds of wit and passion from madness; writing more novels, burning her hero's effigy and letters, and then clamouring for a lock of his hair, or a sight of his portrait; separated from, and again reconciled to, a husband to whose magnanimous forbearance and compassion she bears testimony to the last, comparing herself to Jane Shore; attempting Byronic verses, loudly denouncing and yet never ceasing inwardly to idolize, the man whom she regarded as her betrayer, perhaps only with justice in that he had unwittingly helped to overthrow her mental balance. After eight years of this life, lit up here and there by gleams of social brilliancy, we find her carriage, on the 12th of July, 1824, suddenly confronted by a funeral. On hearing that the remains of Byron were being carried to the tomb, she shrieked, and fainted. Her health finally sank, and her mind gave way under this shock; but she lingered till January, 1828, when she died, after writing a calm letter to her husband, and bequeathing the poet's miniature to her friend, Lady Morgan.

"I have paid some of my debts, and contracted

others," Byron writes to Moore, on September 15th,
1814 ; " but I have a few thousand pounds which I can't
spend after my heart in this climate, and so I shall
go back to the south. I want to see Venice and the
Alps, and Parmesan cheeses, and look at the coast of
Greece from Italy. All this however depends upon an
event which may or may not happen. Whether it will
I shall probably know to-morrow, and if it does I can't
well go abroad at present." " A wife," he had written,
in the January of the same year, "would be my salva-
tion ; " but a marriage entered upon in such a flippant
frame of mind could scarcely have been other than disastrous. In the autumn of the year we are told that a
friend,[2] observing how cheerless was the state both of his
mind and prospects, advised him to marry, and after much
discussion he consented, naming to his correspondent Miss
Milbanke. To this his adviser objected, remarking that she
had, at present, no fortune, and that his embarrassed affairs
would not allow him to marry without one, &c. Accordingly, he agreed that his friend should write a proposal to
another lady, which was done. A refusal arrived as they
were one morning sitting together. " ' You see,' said Lord
Byron, ' that after all Miss Milbanke is to be the person,' and wrote on the moment. His friend, still re-
monstrating against his choice, took up the letter ; but,
on reading it, observed, ' Well, really, this is a very pretty
letter ; it is a pity it should not go.' ' Then it *shall*
go,' said Lord Byron, and, in so saying, sealed and sent
off this fiat of his fate." The incident seems cut from a
French novel; but so does the whole strange story—
the one apparently insoluble enigma in an otherwise
only too transparent life. On the arrival of the lady's

2 Doubtless Moore himself, who tells the story.

answer he was seated at dinner, when his gardener came in, and presented him with his mother's wedding-ring, lost many years before, and which had just been found, buried in the mould beneath her window. Almost at the same moment the letter arrived ; and Byron exclaimed, "If it contains a consent (which it did), I will be married with this very ring." He had the highest anticipations of his bride, appreciating her "talents, and excellent qualities ;" and saying, "she is so good a person that I wish I was a better." About the same date he writes to various friends in the good spirits raised by his enthusiastic reception from the Cambridge undergraduates, when in the course of the same month he went to the Senate House to give his vote for a Professor of Anatomy.

The most constant and best of those friends was his sister, Augusta Leigh, whom, from the death of Miss Chaworth to his own, Byron, in the highest and purest sense of the word, loved more than any other human being. Tolerant of errors, which she lamented, and violences in which she had no share, she had a touch of their common family pride, most conspicuous in an almost cat-like clinging to their ancestral home. Her early published letters are full of regrets about the threatened sale of Newstead, on the adjournment of which, when the first purchaser had to pay 25,000l. for breaking his bargain, she rejoices, and over the consummation of which she mourns, in the manner of Milton's Eve—

Must I then leave thee, Paradise ?

In all her references to the approaching marriage there are blended notes of hope and fear. In thanking Hodgson for his kind congratulations, she trusts it will secure her brother's happiness. Later she adds her testimony to that of all outsiders at this time, as to the graces and

genuine worth of the object of his choice. After the
usual preliminaries, the ill-fated pair were united, at
Seaham House, on the 2nd of January, 1815. Byron
was married like one walking in his sleep. He trembled
like a leaf, made the wrong responses, and almost from
the first seems to have been conscious of his irrevocable
mistake.

> I saw him stand
> Before an altar with a gentle bride :
> Her face was fair, but was not that which made
> The starlight of his boyhood. He could see
> Not that which was—but that which should have been—
> But the old mansion, the accustom'd hall.
> And she who was his destiny came back,
> And thrust herself between him and the light.

Here we have faint visions of Miss Chaworth, mingling
with later memories. In handing the bride into the
carriage he said, "Miss Milbanke, are you ready ?"—a
mistake said to be of evil omen. Byron never really
loved his wife ; and though he has been absurdly accused
of marrying for revenge, we must suspect that he married
in part for a settlement. On the other hand, it is not
unfair to say that she was fascinated by a name, and
inspired by the philanthropic zeal of reforming a literary
Corsair. Both were disappointed. Miss Milbanke's
fortune was mainly settled on herself ; and Byron, in spite
of plentiful resolutions gave little sign of reformation.
For a considerable time their life, which, after the
"treacle moon," as the bridegroom called it, spent at
Halnaby, near Darlington, was divided between residence
at Seaham and visits to London, seemed to move smoothly.
In a letter, evidently mis-dated the 15th December, Mrs.
Leigh writes to Hodgson : " I have every reason to think
that my beloved B. is very happy and comfortable. I hear

constantly from him and *his rib.* It appears to me that
Lady B. sets about making him happy in the right way.
I had many fears. Thank God that they do not appear
likely to be realized. In short, there seems to me to be
but one drawback to all our felicity, and that, alas, is the
disposal of dear Newstead. I never shall feel reconciled
to the loss of that sacred revered Abbey. The thought
makes me more melancholy than perhaps the loss of an
inanimate object ought to do. Did you ever hear
that *landed property,* the GIFT OF THE CROWN, could not
be sold? Lady B. writes me word that she never saw
her father and mother so happy; that she believes the
latter would go to the bottom of the sea herself to find
fish for B.'s dinner, &c." Augusta Ada was born in
London on the 10th of December, 1815. During the
next months a few cynical mutterings are the only
interruptions to an ominous silence ; but these could be
easily explained by the increasing embarrassment of the
poet's affairs, and the importunity of creditors, who in the
course of the last half-year had served seven or eight
executions on his house and furniture. Their expecta-
tions were raised by exaggerated reports of his having
married money ; and by a curious pertinacity of pride he
still declined, even when he had to sell his books, to accept
advances from his publisher. In January the storm
which had been secretly gathering suddenly broke. On
the 15th, i.e. five weeks after her daughter's birth, Lady
Byron left home with the infant to pay a visit, as had
been agreed, to her own family at Kirkby Mallory in
Leicestershire. On the way she despatched to her
husband a tenderly playful letter, which has been often
quoted. Shortly afterwards he was informed—first by
her father, and then by herself—that she did not intend

ever to return to him. The accounts of their last
interview, as in the whole evidence bearing on the
affair, not only differ but flatly contradict one another.
On behalf of Lord Byron it is asserted, that his wife,
infuriated by his offering some innocent hospitality on
occasion of bad weather to a respectable actress, Mrs.
Mardyn, who had called on him about Drury Lane business, rushed into the room exclaiming, " I leave you for
ever"—and did so. According to another story, Lady
Byron, finding him with a friend, and observing him to
be annoyed at her entrance, said, "Am I in your way,
Byron?" whereupon he answered, "Damnably." Mrs.
Leigh, Hodgson, Moore, and others, did everything that
mutual friends could do to bring about the reconciliation
for which Byron himself professed to be eager, but in vain ;
and in vain the effort was renewed in later years. The
wife was inveterately bent on a separation, of the causes
of which the husband alleged he was never informed, and
with regard to which as long as he lived she preserved a
rigid silence.

For some time after the event Byron spoke of his wife
with at least apparent generosity. Rightly or wrongly,
he blamed her parents, and her maid—Mrs. Clermont, the
theme of his scathing but not always dignified " Sketch ;"
but of herself he wrote (March 8, 1816), " I do not believe
that there ever was a brighter, and a kinder, or a more
amiable or agreeable being than Lady Byron. I never
had nor can have any reproach to make to her, when with
me." Elsewhere he adds, that he would willingly, if he
had the chance, " renew his marriage on a lease of twenty
years." But as time passed and his overtures were rejected,
his patience gave way, and in some of his later satires he
even broke the bounds of courtesy. Lady Byron's letters

at the time of the separation, especially those first published in the *Academy* of July 19, 1879, are to Mrs.
Leigh always affectionate and confidential, often pathetic,
asking her advice "in this critical moment," and protesting that, "independent of malady, she does not think
of the past with any spirit of resentment, and scarcely
with the sense of injury." In her communications to
Mr. Hodgson, on the other hand—the first of almost the
same date, the second a few weeks later—she writes with
intense bitterness, stating that her action was due to
offences which she could only condone on the supposition
of her husband's insanity, and distinctly implying that
she was in danger of her life. This supposition having
been by her medical advisers pronounced erroneous, she
felt, in the words only too pungently recalled in *Don
Juan*, that her duty both to man and God prescribed
her course of action. Her playful letter on leaving she
seems to defend on the ground of the fear of personal
violence. Till Lord Byron's death the intimacy between
his wife and sister remained unbroken ; through the latter
he continued to send numerous messages to the former,
and to his child, who became a ward in Chancery ; but at
a later date it began to cool. On the appearance of
Lady Byron's letter, in answer to Moore's first volume,
Augusta speaks of it as "a despicable tirade," feels
"disgusted at such unfeeling conduct," and thinks
"nothing can justify any one in defaming the dead."
Soon after 1830 they had an open rupture on a matter of
business, which was never really healed, though the then
Puritanic precisian sent a message of relenting to Mrs.
Leigh on her death-bed (1851).

The charge or charges which, during her husband's life,
Lady Byron from magnanimity or other motive reserved,

H

she is ascertained after his death to have delivered with
important modifications to various persons, with little
regard to their capacity for reading evidence or to their
discretion. On one occasion her choice of a confidante was
singularly unfortunate. " These," wrote Lord Byron in
his youth, " these are the first tidings that have ever
sounded like fame in my ears—to be redde on the banks of
the Ohio." Strangely enough, it is from the country of
Washington, whom the poet was wont to reverence as the
purest patriot of the modern world, that in 1869 there
emanated the hideous story which scandalized both conti-
nents, and ultimately recoiled on the retailer of the scandal.
The grounds of the reckless charge have been weighed by
those who have wished it to prove false, and by those who
have wished it to prove true, and found wanting. The
chaff has been beaten in every way and on all sides, without
yielding a particle of grain ; and it were ill-advised to rake
up the noxious dust that alone remains. From nothing left
on record by either of the two persons most intimately concerned can we derive any reliable information. It is plain
that Lady Byron was during the later years of her life
the victim of hallucinations, and that if Byron knew the
secret, which he denies, he did not choose to tell it, putting off Captain Medwin and others with absurdities, as
that " He did not like to see women eat," or with commonplaces, as " The causes, my dear sir, were too simple to be
found out."

Thomas Moore, who had the Memoirs [1] supposed
to have thrown light on the mystery, in the full
knowledge of Dr. Lushington's judgment and all the
gossip of the day, professes to believe that " the causes of
disunion did not differ from those that loosen the links

[1] Captain Trelawney, however, doubts if he ever read them.

of most such marriages," and writes several pages on the
trite theme that great genius is incompatible with
domestic happiness. Negative instances abound to
modify this sweeping generalization; but there is a kind
of genius, closely associated with intense irritability,
which it is difficult to subject to the most reasonable yoke;
and of this sort was Byron's. His valet, Fletcher, is reported to have said that "Any woman could manage my
lord, except my lady;" and Madame De Staël, on reading
the *Farewell*, that "She would have been glad to have
been in Lady Byron's place." But it may be doubted if
Byron would have made a good husband to any woman;
his wife and he were even more than usually ill-assorted.
A model of the proprieties, and a pattern of the learned
philanthropy of which in her sex he was wont to make
a constant butt, she was no fit consort for that "mens
insana in corpore insano." What could her placid temperament conjecture of a man whom she saw, in one of
his fits of passion, throwing a favourite watch under the
fire, and grinding it to pieces with a poker? Or how could
her conscious virtue tolerate the recurring irregularities
which he was accustomed, not only to permit himself,
but to parade? The harassment of his affairs stimulated
his violence, till she was inclined to suspect him to be mad.
Some of her recently printed letters—as that to Lady
Anne Barnard, and the reports of later observers
of her character — as William Howitt, tend to detract
from the earlier tributes to her consistent amiability, and
confirm our ideas of the incompatibility of the pair.
It must have been trying to a poet to be asked by his
wife, impatient of his late hours, when he was going
to leave off writing verses; to be told he had no real
enthusiasm; or to have his desk broken open, and its

compromising contents sent to the persons for whom they
were least intended. The smouldering elements of discontent may have been fanned by the gossip of dependants,
or the officious zeal of relatives, and kindled into a jealous
flame by the ostentation of regard for others beyond the
circle of his home. Lady Byron doubtless believed some
story which, when communicated to her legal advisers, led
them to the conclusion that the mere fact of her believing
it made reconciliation impossible ; and the inveterate ob-
stinacy which lurked beneath her gracious exterior, made
her cling through life to the substance—not always to
the form, whatever that may have been—of her first
impressions. Her later letters to Mrs. Leigh, as that
called forth by Moore's *Life*, are certainly as open to the
charge of self-righteousness, as those of her husband's are
to self-disparagement.

Byron himself somewhere says, " Strength of endurance
is worth all the talent in the world." " I love the virtues
that I cannot share." His own courage was all active ; he
had no power of sustained endurance. At a time when his
proper refuge was silence, and his prevailing sentiment—
for he admits he was somehow to blame—should have
been remorse, he foolishly vented his anger and his grief
in verses, most of them either peevish or vindictive, and
some of which he certainly permitted to be published.
" Woe to him," exclaims Voltaire, " who says all he
could on any subject ! " Woe to him, he might have added,
who says anything at all on the subject of his domestic
troubles ! The poet's want of reticence at this crisis
started a host of conjectures, accusations, and calumnies,
the outcome, in some degree at least, of the rancorous
jealousy of men with whose adulation he was weary.
Then began that burst of British virtue on which

Macaulay has expatiated, and at which the social critics
of the continent have laughed.  Cottle, Cato, Oxoniensis,
Delia, and Styles, were let loose, and they anticipated
the *Saturday* and the *Spectator* of 1869, so that the
latter might well have exclaimed, " Pereant qui ante
nos nostra dixerunt." Byron was accused of every
possible and impossible vice. He was compared to
Sardanapalus, Nero, Tiberius, the Duke of Orleans,
Heliogabalus, and Satan—all the most disreputable persons mentioned in sacred and profane history ; his benevolences were maligned, his most disinterested actions
perverted. Mrs. Mardyn, the actress, was on his account,
on one occasion, driven off the public stage.  He was
advised not to go to the theatres, lest he should be
hissed ; nor to Parliament, lest he should be insulted. On
the very day of his departure a friend told him that
he feared violence from mobs assembling at the door of
his carriage.  " Upon what grounds," the poet writes, in
an incisive survey of the circumstances, in August, 1819,
" the public formed their opinion, I am not aware ; but
it was general, and it was decisive.  Of me and of mine
they knew little, except that I had written poetry, was
a nobleman, had married, became a father, and was involved in differences with my wife and her relatives—no
one knew why, because the persons complaining refused
to state their grievances.

" The press was active and scurrilous ; . . . my name
—which had been a knightly or a noble one since
my fathers helped to conquer the kingdom for William the Norman—was tainted. I felt that, if what
was whispered and muttered and murmured was true,
I was unfit for England ; if false, England was unfit
for me. I withdrew ; but this was not enough. In

other countries — in Switzerland, in the shadow of
the Alps, and by the blue depth of the lakes—I was
pursued and breathed upon by the same blight. I
crossed the mountains, but it was the same ; so I went
a little farther, and settled myself by the waves of the
Adriatic, like the stag at bay, who betakes himself to
the waters."

On the 16th of April, 1816, shortly before his departure, he wrote to Mr. Rogers : " My sister is now with
me, and leaves town to-morrow. We shall not meet again
for some time, at all events, if ever (it was their final
meeting), and under these circumstances I trust to
stand excused to you and Mr. Sheridan for being unable
to wait upon him this evening." In all this storm and
stress, Byron's one refuge was in the affection which rises
like a well of purity amid the passions of his turbid
life.

> In the desert a fountain is springing,
> In the wild waste there still is a tree;
> And a bird in the solitude singing,
> That speaks to my spirit of thee.

The fashionable world was tired of its spoilt child,
and he of it. Hunted out of the country, bankrupt in
purse and heart, he left it, never to return ; but he left
it to find fresh inspiration by the " rushing of the arrowy
Rhone," and under Italian skies to write the works
which have immortalized his name.

Earl Spencer.  Sir Ralph Milbanke.  Viscount Wentworth.

F. Ponsonby (Earl of Bessborough). + Henrietta Frances.

Elizabeth (Lady Melbourne) m. Viscount Melbourne.

Sir Ralph + Judith Noel.

Lady Caroline. + William Lamb.

Lord Byron + Anna Isabella.

Augusta Ada.

DESCENT OF ALLEGRA.

William Godwin. Married, 1st. + Mary Woolstonecraft. She had by previous alliance

2nd. Mrs. Clairmont.

P. B. Shelley + Mary Godwin.  Fanny Imlay.  Claire Clairmont + Byron.

Allegra.

## CHAPTER VII.

LIFE ABROAD.—SWITZERLAND TO VENICE.—THIRD PERIOD OF
AUTHORSHIP.—CHILDE HAROLD, III., IV.—MANFRED.

ON the 25th of April, 1816, Byron embarked for Ostend.
From the "burning marl" of the staring streets he planted
his foot again on the deck with a genuine exultation.

> Once more upon the waters, yet once more,
> And the waves bound beneath me as a steed
> That knows her rider. Welcome to the roar!

But he brought with him a relic of English extravagance,
setting out on his land travels in a huge coach, copied
from that of Napoleon taken at Genappe, and being
accompanied by Fletcher, Rushton, Berger, a Swiss, and
an Italian physician called Polidori, son of Alfieri's secre-
tary, a man of some talent but fatal conceit. A question
arises as to the source from which he obtained the means
for these and subsequent luxuries, in striking contrast
with Goldsmith's walking-stick, knapsack, and flute.
Byron's financial affairs are almost inextricably confused.
We can, for instance, nowhere find a clear statement of
the result of the suit regarding the Rochdale Estates,
save that he lost it before the Court of Exchequer, and
that his appeal to the House of Lords was still unsettled
in 1822. The sale of Newstead to Colonel Wildman in
1818, for 90,000l., went mostly to pay off mortgages and

debts. In April, 1819, Mrs. Leigh writes, after a last
sigh over this event :—" Sixty thousand pounds was
secured by his (Byron's) marriage settlement, the interest of which he receives for life, and which ought to
make him very comfortable." This is unfortunately decisive of the fact that he did not in spirit adhere to the
resolution expressed to Moore never to touch a farthing of
his wife's money, though we may accept his statement to
Medwin, that he twice repaid the dowry of 10,000*l.*
brought to him at the marriage, as in so far diminishing
the obligation. None of the capital of Lady Byron's
family came under his control till 1822, when, on the
death of her mother, Lady Noel, Byron arranged the
appointment of referees, Sir Francis Burdett on his
behalf, Lord Dacre on his wife's. The result was an
equal division of a property worth about 7000*l.* a year.
While in Italy the poet received besides about 10,000*l.*
for his writings—4000*l.* being given for *Childe Harold*
(iii., iv.), and *Manfred.* " Ne pas être dupe " was one
of his determinations, and, though he began by caring
little for making money, he was always fond of spending
it. " I tell you it is too much," he said to Murray, in
returning a thousand guineas for the *Corinth* and *Parisina.* Hodgson, Moore, Bland, Thomas Ashe, the family
of Lord Falkland, the British Consul at Venice, and
a host of others, were ready to testify to his superb
munificence. On the other hand, he would stint his
pleasures, or his benevolences, which were among them,
for no one; and when he found that to spend money
he had to make it, he saw neither rhyme nor reason in
accepting less than his due. In 1817 he begins to dun
Murray, declaring, with a frankness in which we can
find no fault, " You offer 1500 guineas for the new canto

(*C. H.*, iv.).  I won't take it.  I ask 2500 guineas for
it, which you will either give or not, as you think
proper." During the remaining years of his life he grew
more and more exact, driving hard bargains for his houses,
horses, and boats, and fitting himself, had he lived, to be
Chancellor of the Exchequer in the newly-liberated State,
from which he took a bond securing a fair interest for
his loan.  He made out an account in £. *s. d.* against
the ungrateful Dallas, and when Leigh Hunt threatened
to sponge upon him he got a harsh reception ; but there
is nothing to countenance the view that Byron was ever
really possessed by the "good old gentlemanly vice" of
which he wrote.  The Skimpoles and Chadbands of the
world are always inclined to talk of filthy lucre : it
is equally a fashion of really lavish people to boast that
they are good men of business.

We have only a few glimpses of Byron's progress.  At
Brussels the Napoleonic coach was set aside for a more
serviceable caleche.  During his stay in the Belgian
capital he paid a visit to the scene of Waterloo, wrote
the famous stanzas beginning, "Stop, for thy tread is
on an empire's dust!" and in unpatriotic prose, recorded
his impressions of a plain which appeared to him to
"want little but a better cause" to make it vie in interest
with those of Platea and Marathon.

The rest of his journey lay up the Rhine to Basle, thence
to Berne, Lausanne, and Geneva, where he settled for a
time at the Hôtel Secheron, on the western shore of the
lake.  Here began the most interesting literary relationship
of his life, for here he first came in contact with the impassioned Ariel of English verse, Percy Bysshe Shelley.
They lived in proximity after they left the hotel, Shelley's
headquarters being at Mont Alégre, and Byron's for the

remainder of the summer at the Villa Diodati; and their
acquaintance rapidly ripened into an intimacy which, with
some interruptions, extended over the six remaining years
of their joint lives. The place for an estimate of their
mutual influence belongs to the time of their Italian part-
nership. Meanwhile, we hear of them mainly as fellow-
excursionists about the lake, which on one occasion depart-
ing from its placid poetical character, all but swallowed
them both, along with Hobhouse, off Meillerie. "The
boat," says Byron, "was nearly wrecked near the very
spot where St. Preux and Julia were in danger of being
drowned. It would have been classical to have been lost
there, but not agreeable. I ran no risk, being so near the
rocks and a good swimmer; but our party were wet and
incommoded." The only anxiety of Shelley, who could
not swim, was, that no one else should risk a life for his.
Two such revolutionary or such brave poets were, in all
probability, never before nor since in a storm in a boat
together. During this period Byron complains of being
still persecuted. "I was in a wretched state of health and
worse spirits when I was in Geneva; but quiet and the
lake—better physicians than Polidori—soon set me up.
I never led so moral a life as during my residence in that
country, but I gained no credit by it. On the contrary,
there is no story so absurd that they did not invent at my
cost. I was watched by glasses on the opposite side of the
lake, and by glasses, too, that must have had very distorted
optics. I was waylaid in my evening drives. I believe
they looked upon me as a man-monster." Shortly after
his arrival in Switzerland he contracted an intimacy with
Miss Clairmont, a daughter of Godwin's second wife, and
consequently a connexion by marriage of the Shelleys,
with whom she was living, which resulted in the birth of

a daughter, Allegra, at Great Marlow, in February, 1817.
The noticeable events of the following two months are
a joint excursion to Chamouni, and a visit in July to
Madame de Staël at Coppet, in the course of which he met
Frederick Schlegel. During a wet week, when the families
were reading together some German ghost stories, an idea
occurred of imitating them, the main result of which was
Mrs. Shelley's *Frankenstein.* Byron contributed to the
scheme a fragment of *The Vampire,* afterwards completed
and published in the name of his patron by Polidori.
This eccentric physician now began to develope a vein of
half insanity : his jealousy of Shelley grew to such a pitch
that it resulted in the doctor's sending a challenge to the
poet. Shelley only laughed at this ; but Byron, to stop
further impertinences of the kind, remarked, " Recollect
that, though Shelley has scruples about duelling, I have
none, and shall be at all times ready to take his place."
Polidori had ultimately to be dismissed, and, after some
years of absurd adventure, committed suicide.

The Shelleys left for England in September, and
Byron made an excursion with Hobhouse through the
Bernese Oberland. They went by the Col de Jaman
and the Simmenthal to Thun ; then up the valley to the
Staubbach, which he compares to the tail of the pale
horse in the Apocalypse—not a very happy, though a
striking comparison. Thence they proceeded over the
Wengern to Grindelwald and the Rosenlau glacier ; then
back by Berne, Friburg, and Yverdun to Diodati. The
following passage in reference to this tour may be selected
as a specimen of his prose description, and of the ideas
of mountaineering before the days of the Alpine Club :—

" Before ascending the mountain, went to the torrent
again, the sun upon it forming a rainbow of the lower

part, of all colours but principally purple and gold, the
bow moving as you move. I never saw anything like
this; it is only in the sunshine. . . . . Left the horses,
took off my coat, and went to the summit, 7000 English
feet above the level of the sea, and 5000 feet above the
valley we left in the morning. On one side our view
comprised the Jungfrau, with all her glaciers; then the
Dent d'Argent, shining like truth; then the Eighers and
the Wetterhorn. Heard the avalanches falling every five
minutes. From where we stood on the Wengern Alp we
had all these in view on one side; on the other, the
clouds rose up from the opposite valley, curling up per-
pendicular precipices, like the foam of the ocean of hell
during a spring tide; it was white and sulphury, and
immeasurably deep in appearance. . . . . Arrived at the
Grindelwald; dined; mounted again, and rode to the
higher glacier—like a frozen hurricane; starlight beautiful,
but a devil of a path. Passed whole woods of withered
pines, all withered; trunks stripped and barkless, branches
lifeless; done by a single winter. Their appearance reminded me of me and my family."

Students of *Manfred* will recognize whole sentences,
only slightly modified in its verse. Though Byron talks
with contempt of authorship, there is scarce a fine phrase
in his letters or journal which is not pressed into the
author's service. He turns his deepest griefs to artistic
gain, and uses five or six times for literary purposes the
expression which seems to have dropped from him naturally about his household gods being shivered on his
hearth. His account of this excursion concludes with
a passage equally characteristic of his melancholy and
incessant self-consciousness :—

"In the weather for this tour, I have been very

fortunate. . . . . I was disposed to be pleased.  I am a
lover of nature, &c. . . . . But in all this the recollection of bitterness, and more especially of recent and more
home desolation, which must accompany me through life,
have preyed upon me here ; and neither the music of the
shepherd, the crashing of the avalanche, the torrent, the
mountain, the glacier, the forest, nor the cloud, have for
one moment lightened the weight upon my heart, nor
enabled me to lose my own wretched identity in the
majesty, and the power, and the glory around, above, and
beneath me."

Such egotism in an idle man would only provoke impatience ; but Byron was, during the whole of this period,
almost preternaturally active.  Detained by bad weather
at Ouchy for two days (June 26, 27), he wrote the *Prisoner
of Chillon*, which, with its noble introductory sonnet on
Bonnivard, in some respects surpasses any of his early
romances.  The opening lines,—

> Lake Leman lies by Chillon's walls ;
> A thousand feet in depth below,
> Its massy waters meet and flow,—

bring before us in a few words the conditions of a hope-
less bondage.  The account of the prisoner himself, and of
the lingering deaths of the brothers ; the first frenzy of the
survivor, and the desolation which succeeds it—

> I only loved : I only drew
> The accursed breath of dungeon dew,—

the bird's song breaking on the night of his solitude ; his
growing enamoured of despair, and regaining his freedom
with a sigh, are all strokes from a master hand.  From
the same place, at the same date, he announces to
Murray the completion of the third canto of *Childe*

*Harold.* The productiveness of July is portentous. During that month he wrote the *Monody on Sheridan, The Dream, Churchill's Grave,* the *Sonnet to Lake Leman, Could I remount the River of my Years,* part of *Manfred, Prometheus,* the *Stanzas to Augusta,* beginning,

> My sister ! My sweet sister ! If a name
> Dearer and purer were, it should be thine ;

and the terrible dream of *Darkness,* which at least in the ghastly power of the close, where the survivors meet by the lurid light of a dim altar fire, and die of each other's hideousness, surpasses Campbell's *Last Man.*[1]  At Lausanne the poet made a pilgrimage to the haunts of Gibbon, broke a sprig from his acacia-tree, and carried off some rose leaves from his garden.  Though entertaining friends, among them Mr. M. G. Lewis and Scrope Davies, he systematically shunned "the locust swarm of English tourists," remarking on their obtrusive platitudes ; as when he heard one of them at Chamouni inquire, "Did you ever see anything more truly rural ?"  Ultimately he got tired of the Calvinistic Genevese—one of whom is said to have swooned as he entered the room—and early in October set out with Hobhouse for Italy. They crossed the Simplon, and proceeded by the Lago Maggiore to Milan, admiring the pass, but slighting the somewhat hothouse beauties of the Borromean Islands. From Milan he writes, pronouncing its cathedral to be only a little inferior to that of Seville, and delighted with "a correspondence, all original and amatory, between Lucretia Borgia and Cardinal Bembo."  He

---

[1] This only appeared in 1831, but Campbell claims to have given Byron in conversation the suggestion of the subject.

secured a lock of the golden hair of the Pope's
daughter, and wished himself a cardinal.

At Verona, Byron dilates on the amphitheatre, as
surpassing anything he had seen even in Greece, and
on the faith of the people in the story of Juliet, from
whose reputed tomb he sent some pieces of granite to
Ada and his nieces. In November we find him settled
in Venice, " the greenest isle of his imagination." There
he began to form those questionable alliances which are
so marked a feature of his life, and so frequent a theme
in his letters, that it is impossible to pass them without
notice. The first of his temporary idols was Mariana
Segati, " the wife of a merchant of Venice," for some time
his landlord. With this woman, whom he describes as an
antelope with oriental eyes, wavy hair, a voice like the
cooing of a dove, and the spirit of a Bacchante, he
remained on terms of intimacy for about eighteen
months, during which their mutual devotion was only
disturbed by some outbursts of jealousy. In December
the poet took lessons in Armenian, glad to find in
the study something craggy to break his mind upon.
He translated into that language a portion of St. Paul's
Epistle to the Corinthians. Notes on the carnival,
praises of *Christabel*, instructions about the printing
of *Childe Harold* (iii.), protests against the publication
under his name of some spurious " domestic poems,"
and constant references, doubtfully domestic, to his
Adriatic lady, fill up the records of 1816. On February
15, 1817, he announces to Murray the completion
of the first sketch of *Manfred*, and alludes to it in a
bantering manner as " a kind of poem in dialogue, of a
wild metaphysical and inexplicable kind ; " concluding,
" I have at least rendered it *quite impossible* for the

stage, for which my intercourse with Drury Lane has given me the greatest contempt."

About this time Byron seems to have entertained the idea of returning to England in the spring, i. e. after a year's absence. This design, however, was soon set aside, partly in consequence of a slow malarial fever, by which he was prostrated for several weeks. On his partial recovery, attributed to his having had neither medicine nor doctor, and a determination to live till he had " put one or two people out of the world," he started on an expedition to Rome.

His first stage was Arqua; then Ferrara, where he was inspired, by a sight of the Italian poet's prison, with the *Lament of Tasso ;* the next, Florence, where he describes himself as drunk with the beauty of the galleries. Among the pictures, he was most impressed with the mistresses of Raphael and Titian, to whom, along with Giorgione, he is always reverential; and he recognized in Santa Croce the Westminster Abbey of Italy. Passing through Foligno, he reached his destination early in May, and met his old friends, Lord Lansdowne and Hobhouse. The poet employed his short time at Rome in visiting on horseback the most famous sites in the city and neighbourhood—as the Alban Mount, Tivoli, Frascati, the Falls of Terni, and the Clitumnus—re-casting the crude first draft of the third act of *Manfred*, and sitting for his bust to Thorwaldsen. Of this sitting the sculptor afterwards gave some account to his compatriot, Hans Andersen : " Byron placed himself opposite to me, but at once began to put on a quite different expression from that usual to him. ' Will you not sit still ?' said I. ' You need not assume that look.' ' That is my expression,' said Byron. ' Indeed,' said I ; and I then

I

represented him as I wished. When the bust was
finished he said, ' It is not at all like me ; my expression
is more unhappy.'" West, the American, who five years
later painted his lordship at Leghorn, substantiates the
above half-satirical anecdote, by the remark, " He was a
bad sitter ; he assumed a countenance that did not belong
to him, as though he were thinking of a frontispiece for
*Childe Harold.*" Thorwaldsen's bust, the first cast of
which was sent to Hobhouse, and pronounced by Mrs.
Leigh to be the best of the numerous likenesses of her
brother, was often repeated. Professor Brandes, of
Copenhagen, introduces his striking sketch of the
poet by a reference to the model, that has its natural
place in the museum named from the great sculptor
whose genius had flung into the clay the features of a
character so unlike his own. The bust, says the Danish
critic, at first sight impresses one with an undefin-
able classic grace ; on closer examination the restlessness
of a life is reflected in a brow over which clouds seem to
hover, but clouds from which we look for lightnings.
The dominant impression of the whole is that of some
irresistible power (Unwiderstehlichkeit). Thorwaldsen,
at a much later date (1829—1833) executed the marble
statue, first intended for the Abbey, which is now to be
seen in the library of Trinity College, in evidence that
Cambridge is still proud of her most brilliant son.

Towards the close of the month—after almost fainting
at the execution by guillotine of three bandits—he professes impatience to get back to Mariana, and early in
the next we find him established with her near Venice,
at the villa of La Mira, where for some time he continued to reside. His letters of June refer to the sale of
Newstead, the mistake of Mrs. Leigh and others in

attributing to him the *Tales of a Landlord*, the appearance of *Lalla Rookh*, preparations for *Marino Faliero*, and the progress of *Childe Harold* iv. This poem, completed in September, and published early in 1818 (with a dedication to Hobhouse, who had supplied most of the illustrative notes), first made manifest the range of the poet's power. Only another slope of ascent lay between him and the pinnacle, over which shines the red star of *Cain*. Had Lord Byron's public career closed when he left England, he would have been remembered for a generation as the author of some musical minor verses, a clever satire, a journal in verse exhibiting flashes of genius, and a series of fascinating romances— also giving promise of higher power—which had enjoyed a marvellous popularity. The third and fourth cantos of *Childe Harold* placed him on another platform, that of the *Dii Majores* of English verse. These cantos are separated from their predecessors, not by a stage, but by a gulf. Previous to their publication he had only shown how far the force of rhapsody could go; now he struck with his right hand, and from the shoulder. Knowledge of life and study of Nature were the mainsprings of a growth which the indirect influence of Wordsworth, and the happy companionship of Shelley, played their part in fostering. Faultlessness is seldom a characteristic of impetuous verse, never of Byron's; and even in the later parts of the *Childe* there are careless lines, and doubtful images. " Self-exiled Harold wanders forth again," looking " pale and interesting ; " but we are soon refreshed by a higher note. No familiarity can detract from " Waterloo," which holds its own by Barbour's " Bannockburn," and Scott's " Flodden." Sir Walter, referring to the climax of the opening, and the pathetic

lament of the closing lines, generously doubts whether
any verses in English surpass them in vigour. There
follows "The Broken Mirror," extolled by Jeffrey with
an appreciation of its exuberance of fancy, and negligence
of diction; and then the masterly sketch of Napoleon,
with the implied reference to the writer at the end.

The descriptions in both cantos perpetually rise
from a basis of rhetoric to a real height of poetry.
Byron's "Rhine" flows, like the river itself, in a stream of
"exulting and abounding" stanzas. His "Venice" may be
set beside the masterpieces of Ruskin's prose. They are
together the joint pride of Italy and England. The
tempest in the third canto is in verse a splendid
microcosm of the favourite, if not the prevailing mood,
of the writer's mind. In spite of manifest flaws, the nine
stanzas beginning "It is the hush of night," have enough
in them to feed a high reputation. The poet's dying
day, his sun and moon contending over the Rhœtian
hill, his Thrasymene, Clitumnus, and Velino, show that
his eye has grown keener, and his imagery at least more
terse, and that he can occasionally forget himself in his
surroundings. The Drachenfells, Ehrenbreitstein, the
Alps, Lake Leman, pass before us like a series of
dissolving views. But the stability of the book depends
on its being a Temple of Fame, as well as a Diorama of
Scenery. It is no mere versified Guide, because every
resting-place in the pilgrimage is made interesting by
association with illustrious memories. Coblentz introduces the tribute to Marceau; Clarens an almost complete
review, in five verses, of Rousseau; Lausanne and Ferney
the quintessence of criticism on Gibbon and Voltaire.
A tomb in Arqua suggests Petrarch; the grass-grown
streets of Ferrara lead in the lines on Tasso; the white

walls of the Etrurian Athens bring back Alfieri and
Michael Angelo, and the prose bard of the hundred tales,
and Dante, "buried by the upbraiding shore," and—

The starry Galileo and his woes.

Byron has made himself so master of the glories and
the wrecks of Rome, that almost everything else that has
been said of them seems superfluous. Hawthorne, in his
*Marble Fawn*, comes nearest to him; but Byron's
Gladiator and Apollo, if not his Laocoon, are unequalled.
"The voice of Marius," says Scott, "could not sound more
deep and solemn among the ruins of Carthage, than the
strains of the pilgrim among the broken shrines and
fallen statues of her subduer." As the third canto has a
fitting close with the poet's pathetic remembrance of his
daughter, so the fourth is wound up with consummate
art,—the memorable dirge on the Princess Charlotte being
followed by the address to the sea, which, enduring un-
wrinkled through all its ebbs and flows, seems to mock
at the mutability of human life.

*Manfred*, his witch drama, as the author called it,
has had a special attraction for inquisitive biographers,
because it has been supposed in some dark manner to
reveal the secrets of his prison house. Its lines have been
tortured, like the witches of the seventeenth century, to
extort from them the meaning of the "all nameless hour,"
and every conceivable horror has been alleged as its
*motif*. On this subject Goethe writes with a humorous
simplicity : " This singularly intellectual poet has ex-
tracted from my *Faust* the strongest nourishment for his
hypochondria ; but he has made use of the impelling
principles for his own purposes. . . When a bold and
enterprising young man, he won the affections of a

Florentine lady. Her husband discovered the amour, and murdered his wife; but the murderer was the same night found dead in the street, and there was no one to whom any suspicion could be attached. Lord Byron removed from Florence, but these spirits have haunted him all his life. This romantic incident explains innumerable allusions," e. g.,—

> I have shed
> Blood, but not hers,—and yet her blood was shed.

Were it not for the fact that the poet had never seen the city in question when he wrote the poem, this explanation would be more plausible than most others, for the allusions are all to some lady who has been done to death. Galt asserts that the plot turns on a tradition of unhallowed necromancy—a human sacrifice, like that of Antinous attributed to Hadrian. Byron himself says it has no plot, but he kept teasing his questioners with mysterious hints, e. g. " It was the Staubbach and the Jungfrau, and something else more than Faustus, which made me write *Manfred*; " and of one of his critics he says to Murray, " It had a better origin than he can devise or divine, for the soul of him." In any case most methods of reading between its lines would, if similarly applied, convict Sophocles, Schiller, and Shelley of incest, Shakespeare of murder, Milton of blasphemy, Scott of forgery, Marlowe and Goethe of compacts with the devil. Byron was no dramatist, but he had wit enough to vary at least the circumstances of his projected personality. The memories of both Fausts—the Elizabethan and the German—mingle, in the pages of this piece, with shadows of the author's life; but to these it never gives, nor could be intended to give, any substantial form.

*Manfred* is a chaos of pictures, suggested by the

scenery of Lauterbrunnen and Grindelwald, half animated
by vague personifications and sensational narrative.   Like
*Harold*, and Scott's *Marmion*, it just misses being a great
poem.   The Coliseum is its masterpiece of description,
the appeal, " Astarte, my beloved, speak to me," its
nearest approach to pathos.   The lonely death of the hero
makes an effective close to the moral tumult of the preceding scenes.   But the reflections, often striking, are
seldom absolutely fresh : that beginning,

> The mind, which is immortal, makes itself
> Requital for its good or evil thoughts,
> Is its own origin of ill and end,
> And its own place and time,

is transplanted from Milton with as little change as
Milton made in transplanting it from Marlowe.   The
author's own favourite passage, the invocation to the sun
(act iii., sc. 2), has some sublimity, marred by lapses.
The lyrics scattered through the poem sometimes open
well, e. g.,—

> Mont Blanc is the monarch of mountains ;
> They crowned him long ago,
> On a throne of rocks, in a robe of clouds,
> With a diadem of snow ;

but they cannot sustain themselves like true song-birds,
and fall to the ground like spent rockets.   This applies
to Byron's lyrics generally ; turn to the incantation in
the *Deformed Transformed* : the first two lines are in
tune,—

> Beautiful shadow of Thetis's boy,
> Who sleeps in the meadow whose grass grows o'er Troy.

Nor Sternhold nor Hopkins has more ruthlessly out-
raged our ears than the next two —

From the red earth, like Adam, thy likeness I shape,
As the Being who made him, whose actions I ape (!)

Of his songs : " There be none of Beauty's daughters,"
" She walks in beauty," " Maid of Athens," " I enter thy
garden of roses," the translation " Sons of the Greeks,"
and others, have a flow and verve that it is pedantry
to ignore ; but in general Byron was too much of the earth
earthy to be a great lyrist.    Some of the greatest have
lived wild lives, but their wings were not weighted with
the lead of the love of the world.

The summer and early months of the autumn of 1817
were spent at La Mira, and much of the poet's time was
occupied in riding along the banks of the Brenta, often
in the company of the few congenial Englishmen who
came in his way ; others, whom he avoided, avenged
themselves by retailing stories, none of which were " too
improbable for the craving appetites of their slander-
loving countrymen."    In August he received a visit
from Mr. Hobhouse, and on this occasion drew up the
remarkable document afterwards given to Mr. M. G.
Lewis for circulation in England, which appeared in the
*Academy* of October 9th, 1869.    In this document he
says, " It has been intimated to me that the persons under-
stood to be the legal advisers of Lady Byron have declared
their lips to be sealed up on the cause of the separation
between her and myself.    If their lips are sealed up they
are not sealed up by me, and the greatest favour they can
confer upon me will be to open them."    He goes on to
state, that he repents having consented to the separation—
will be glad to cancel the deed, or to go before any
tribunal, to discuss the matter in the most public manner ;
adding, that Mr. Hobhouse (in whose presence he was
writing) proposed, on his part, to go into court, and

ending with a renewed asseveration of his ignorance of the
allegations against him, and his inability to understand
for what purpose they had been kept back, "unless it
was to sanction the most infamous calumnies by silence."
Hobhouse, and others, during the four succeeding years,
ineffectually endeavoured to persuade the poet to return
to England.  Moore and others insist that Byron's
heart was at home when his presence was abroad,
and that, with all her faults, he loved his country still.
Leigh Hunt, on the contrary, asserts that he cared
nothing for England or its affairs.  Like many men of
genius, Byron was never satisfied with what he had
at the time.  "Romæ Tibur amem ventosus Tibure
Romam."  At Seaham he is bored to death, and pants
for the excitement of the clubs ; in London society he
longs for a desert or island in the Cyclades ; after their
separation, he begins to regret his wife ; after his exile,
his country.  "Where," he exclaimed to Hobhouse,
"is real comfort to be found out of England?"  He
frequently fell into the mood in which he wrote the
verse,—

> Yet I was born where men are proud to be,
> Not without cause : and should I leave behind
> Th' immortal island of the sage and free,
> And seek me out a home by a remoter sea ?

But the following, to Murray (June 7, 1819), is equally
sincere.  "Some of the epitaphs at Ferrara pleased me
more than the more splendid monuments of Bologna ;
for instance—

> ' Martini Luigi
> Implora pace.'

> ' Lucrezia Picini
> Implora eterne quiete.'

Can anything be more full of pathos ?  These few words
say all that can be said or sought; the dead had had
enough of life ; all they wanted was rest, and this they
implore.  There is all the helplessness, and humble hope,
and death-like prayer that can arise from the grave—
'implora pace.'  I hope, whoever may survive me, and
shall see me put in the foreigner's burying-ground at the
Lido, within the fortress by the Adriatic, will see these
two words, and no more, put over me.  I trust they
won't think of pickling and bringing me home to Clod,
or Blunderbuss Hall.  I am sure my bones would not
rest in an English grave, or my clay mix with the earth
of that country."  Hunt's view is, in this as in other
subtle respects, nearer the truth than Moore's ; for with
all Byron's insight into Italian vice, he hated more the
master vice of England—hypocrisy ; and much of his
greatest, and in a sense latest, because unfinished work,
is the severest, as it might be the wholesomest, satire ever
directed against a great nation since the days of Juvenal
and Tacitus.

In September (1817) Byron entered into negotiations,
afterwards completed, for renting a country house among
the Euganean hills near Este, from Mr. Hoppner, the
English Consul at Venice, who bears frequent testimony
to his kindness and courtesy.  In October we find him
settled for the winter in Venice, where he fiɔt occupied
his old quarters, in the Spezieria, and afterwards hired
one of the palaces of the Countess Mocenigo on the
Grand Canal.  Between this mansion, the cottage at Este,
and the villa of La Mira, he divided his time for the next
two years.  During the earlier part of his Venetian career
he had continued to frequent the salon of the Countess
Albrizzi, where he met with people of both sexes of

some rank and standing who appreciated his genius, though some among them fell into absurd mistakes. A gentleman of the company informing the hostess, in answer to some inquiry regarding Canova's busts, that Washington, the American President, was shot in a duel by Burke, " What, in the name of folly, are you thinking of?" said Byron, perceiving that the speaker was confounding Washington with Hamilton, and Burke with Burr. He afterwards transferred himself to the rival coterie of the Countess Benzoni, and gave himself up with little reserve to the intrigues which cast discredit on this portion of his life. Nothing is so conducive to dissipation as despair, and Byron had begun to regard the Sea-Cybele as a Sea-Sodom—when he wrote, " To watch a city die daily, as she does, is a sad contemplation. I sought to distract my mind from a sense of her desolation and my own solitude, by plunging into a vortex that was anything but pleasure." In any case, he forsook the " Dame," and, by what his biographer calls a " descent in the scale of refinement, for which nothing but the wayward state of his mind can account," sought the companions of his leisure hours among the wearers of the " fazzioli." The carnivals of the years 1818, 1819, mark the height of his excesses. Early in the former, Mariana Segati fell out of favour, owing to Byron's having detected her in selling the jewels he had given as presents, and so being led to suspect a large mercenary element in her devotion. To her succeeded Margarita Cogni, the wife of a baker who proved as accommodating as his predecessor, the linen-draper. This woman was decidedly a character, and Señor Castelar has almost elevated her into a heroine. A handsome virago, with brown shoulders, and black hair, endowed with the

strength of an Amazon, "a face like Faustina's, and the
figure of a Juno—tall and energetic as a pythoness,"
she quartered herself for twelve months in the palace
as "Donna di governo," and drove the servants about
without let or hindrance. Unable to read or write
she intercepted his lordship's letters to little purpose;
but she had great natural business talents, reduced by
one half the expenses of his household, kept everything in good order, and, when her violences roused his
wrath, turned it off with some ready retort or witticism.
She was very devout, and would cross herself three times
at the Angelus. One instance, of a different kind of
devotion, from Byron's own account, is sufficiently
graphic :—"In the autumn one day, going to the Lido
with my gondoliers, we were overtaken by a heavy squall,
and the gondola put in peril, hats blown away, boat filling,
oar lost, tumbling sea, thunder, rain in torrents, and
wind unceasing. On our return, after a tight struggle, I
found her on the open steps of the Mocenigo Palace
on the Grand Canal, with her great black eyes flashing
through her tears, and the long dark hair which was
streaming, drenched with rain, over her brows. She was
perfectly exposed to the storm ; and the wind blowing
her dress about her thin figure, and the lightning flashing round her, made her look like Medea alighted from
her chariot, or the Sibyl of the tempest that was rolling
around her, the only living thing within hail at that
moment, except ourselves. On seeing me safe she did
not wait to greet me, as might have been expected ; but,
calling out to me, ' Ah ! can' della Madonna, xe esto il
tempo per andar' al' Lido,' ran into the house, and
solaced herself with scolding the boatmen for not fore-
seeing the ' temporale.' Her joy at seeing me again was

moderately mixed with ferocity, and gave me the idea
of a tigress over her recovered cubs."

Some months after she became ungovernable—threw
plates about, and snatched caps from the heads of
other women who looked at her lord in public places.
Byron told her she must go home; whereupon she proceeded to break glass, and threaten "knives, poison,
fire;" and on his calling his boatmen to get ready the
gondola, threw herself in the dark night into the canal.
She was rescued, and in a few days finally dismissed;
after which he saw her only twice, at the theatre. Her
whole picture is more like that of Théroigne de Méricourt
than that of Raphael's Fornarina, whose name she received.

Other stories, of course, gathered round this strange
life—personal encounters, aquatic feats, and all manner
of romantic and impossible episodes; their basis being,
that Byron on one occasion thrashed, on another challenged, a man who tried to cheat him, was a frequent
rider, and a constant swimmer, so that he came to be
called "the English fish," "water-spaniel," "sea-devil,"
&c. One of the boatmen is reported to have said, "He
is a good gondolier, spoilt by being a poet and a lord;"
and in answer to a traveller's inquiry, "Where does he
get his poetry?" "He dives for it." His habits, as
regards eating, seem to have been generally abstemious;
but he drank a pint of gin and water over his verses
at night, and then took claret and soda in the morning.

Riotous living may have helped to curtail Byron's
life, but it does not seem to have seriously impaired his
powers. Among these adverse surroundings of the "court
of Circe," he threw off *Beppo, Mazeppa,* and the early
books of *Don Juan.* The first canto of the last was

written in November, 1818, the second in January, 1819,
the third and fourth towards the close of the same year.
*Beppo*, its brilliant prelude, sparkles like a draught of
champagne. This " Venetian story," or sketch, in which
the author broke ground on his true satiric field—the
satire of social life—and first adopted the measure avowedly
suggested by Frere's *Whistlecraft*, was drafted in October,
1817, and appeared in May, 1818. It aims at comparatively little, but is perfectly successful in its aim, and
unsurpassed for the incisiveness of its side strokes, and
the courtly ease of a manner that never degenerates into
mannerism. In *Mazeppa* the poet reverts to his earlier
style, and that of Scott ; the description of the headlong
ride hurries us along with a breathless expectancy that
gives it a conspicuous place among his minor efforts.
The passage about the howling of the wolves, and the
fever faint of the victim, is as graphic as anything in
Burns—

> The skies spun like a mighty wheel,
> I saw the trees like drunkards reel.

In the May or June of 1818 Byron's little daughter,
Allegra, had been sent from England, under the care of a
Swiss nurse too young to undertake her management in
such trying circumstances, and after four months of
anxiety he placed her in charge of Mrs. Hoppner.
In the course of this and the next year there are
frequent allusions to the child, all, save one which records a mere affectation of indifference, full of affectionate
solicitude. In June, 1819, he writes, " Her temper and
her ways, Mr. Hoppner says, are like mine, as well as
her features ; she will make, in that case, a manageable
young lady." Later he talks of her as " flourishing like
a pomegranate blossom." In March, 1820, we have

another reference. " Allegra is prettier, I think, but as obstinate as a mule, and as ravenous as a vulture ; health good, to judge by the complexion, temper tolerable, but for vanity and pertinacity. She thinks herself handsome, and will do as she pleases."<sup></sup> In May he refers to having received a letter from her mother, but gives no details. In the following year, with the approval of the Shelleys then at Pisa, he placed her for education in the convent of Cavalli Bagni in the Romagna. " I have," he writes to Hoppner, who had thought of having her boarded in Switzerland, " neither spared care, kindness, nor expense, since the child was sent to me. The people may say what they please. I must content myself with not deserving, in this instance, that they should speak ill. The place is a *country* town, in a good air, and less liable to objections of every kind. It has always appeared to me that the moral defect in Italy does *not* proceed from a *conventual* education ; because, to my certain knowledge, they come out of their convents innocent, even to ignorance of moral evil ; but to the state of society into which they are directly plunged on coming out of it. It is like educating an infant on a mountain top, and then taking him to the sea, and throwing him into it, and desiring him to swim." Elsewhere he says, " I by no means intend to give a natural child an English education, because, with the disadvantages of her birth, her after settlement would be doubly difficult. Abroad, with a fair foreign education, and a portion of 5000*l*. or 6000*l*. (his will leaving her 5000*l*., on condition that she should not marry an Englishman, is here explained and justified), she might, and may, marry very respectably. In England such a dowry would be a pittance, while elsewhere it is a fortune. It is, besides, my wish that

she should be a Roman Catholic, which I look upon as
the best religion, as it is assuredly the oldest of the
various branches of Christianity." It only remains to
add that, when he heard that the child had fallen
ill of fever in 1822, Byron was almost speechless with
agitation, and, on the news of her death, which took
place April 22nd, he seemed at first utterly prostrated.
Next day he said, " Allegra is dead ; she is more fortunate
than we. It is God's will, let us mention it no more."
Her remains rest beneath the elm-tree at Harrow which
her father used to haunt in boyhood, with the date of
birth and death, and the verse—

> I shall go to her, but she shall not return to me.

The most interesting of the visits paid to Byron during the
period of his life at Venice was that of Shelley, who, leaving
his wife and children at Bagni di Lucca, came to see him in
August, 1818. He arrived late, in the midst of a thunderstorm ; and next day they sailed to the Lido, and rode
together along the sands. The attitude of the two poets
towards each other is curious ; the comparatively shrewd
man of the world often relied on the idealist for guidance
and help in practical matters, admired his courage and
independence, spoke of him invariably as the best of men,
but never paid a sufficiently warm tribute in public to his
work. Shelley, on the other hand, certainly the most
modest of great poets, contemplates Byron in the fixed
attitude of a literary worshipper.

The introduction to *Julian and Maddalo*, directly suggested by this visit, under the slight veil of a change in
the name, gives a summary of the view of his friend's
character which he continued to entertain. " He is a person of the most consummate genius, and capable if he

would direct his energies to such an end, of becoming the
redeemer of his degraded country. But it is his weakness to be proud ; he derives, from a comparison of his
own extraordinary mind with the dwarfish intellects that
surround him, an intense apprehension of the nothingness
of human life. His passions and his powers are incomparably greater than those of other men ; and instead of
the latter having been employed in curbing the former,
they have mutually lent each other strength ;" but "in
social life no human being can be more gentle, patient, and
unassuming. He is cheerful, frank, and witty. His
more serious conversation is a sort of intoxication ; men
are held by it as by a spell."

Subsequently to this visit Byron lent the villa at Este
to his friend, and during the autumn weeks of their
residence there were written the lines among the Euganean
hills, where, in the same strain of reverence, Shelley
refers to the "tempest-cleaving swan of Albion," to the
"music flung o'er a mighty thunder-fit," and to the sun-
like soul destined to immortalize his ocean refuge,—

> As the ghost of Homer clings
> Round Scamander's wasting springs,
> As divinest Shakespeare's might
> Fills Avon and the world with light.

"The sun," he says, at a later date, "has extinguished
the glowworm ;" and again, "I despair of rivalling Lord
Byron, as well I may ; and there is no other with whom it
is worth contending."

Shelley was, in the main, not only an exquisite but a
trustworthy critic ; and no man was more absolutely above
being influenced by the fanfaronade of rank or the din
of popularity. These criticisms are therefore not to
be lightly set aside, nor are they unintelligible. Perhaps

K

those admirers of the clearer and more consistent nature,
who exalt him to the rank of a greater poet, are misled by
the amiable love of one of the purest characters in the
history of our literature.  There is at least no difficulty
in understanding why he should have been, as it were,
concussed by Byron's greater massiveness and energy into
a sense—easy to a man half bard, half saint—of inferiority.
Similarly, most of the estimates—many already reversed,
others reversible—by the men of that age, of each other,
can be explained.  We can see how it was that Shelley
overestimated both the character and the powers of Hunt ;
and Byron depreciated Keats, and was ultimately repelled by Wordsworth, and held out his hand to meet
the manly grasp of Scott.  The one enigma of their
criticism is the respect that they joined in paying to the
witty, genial, shallow, worldly, musical Tom Moore.

This favourite of fortune and the minor muses, in the
course of a short tour through the north of Italy in the
autumn of 1819, found his noble friend on the 8th of
October at La Mira, went with him on a sight-seeing
expedition to Venice, and passed five or six days in his
company.  Of this visit he has recorded his impressions,
some of which relate to his host's personal appearance,
others to his habits and leading incidents of his life.
Byron "had grown fatter, both in person and face, and
the latter had suffered most by the change, having lost by
the enlargement of the features some of that refined and
spiritualized look that had in other times distinguished
it, but although less romantic he appeared more
humorous."  They renewed their recollections of the
old days and nights in London, and compared them with
later experiences of Bores and Blues, in a manner which
threatened to put to flight the historical and poetical

associations naturally awakened by the City of the Sea.
Byron had a rooted dislike to any approach to fine talk in
the ordinary intercourse of life ; and when his companion
began to rhapsodize on the rosy hue of the Italian sunsets,
he interrupted him with, " Come, d—n it, Tom, *don't* be
poetical." He insisted on Moore, who sighed after what
he imagined would be the greater comforts of an hotel,
taking up his quarters in his palace ; and as they were
groping their way through the somewhat dingy entrance,
cried out, " Keep clear of the dog ! " and a few paces
farther, " Take care, or the monkey will fly at you !" an
incident recalling the old vagaries of the menagerie at
Newstead. The biographer's reminiscences mainly dwell
on his lordship's changing moods and tempers and gym-
nastic exercises, his terror of interviewing strangers, his
imperfect appreciation of art, his preference of fish to
flesh, his almost parsimonious economy in small matters,
mingled with allusions to his domestic calamities, and
frequent expressions of a growing distaste to Venetian
society. On leaving the city, Moore passed a second afternoon at La Mira, had a glimpse of Allegra, and the first
intimation of the existence of the notorious Memoirs.
" A short time after dinner Byron left the room, and
returned carrying in his hand a white leather bag.
' Look here,' he said, holding it up ; ' this would be
worth something to Murray, though *you*, I dare say,
would not give sixpence for it.' ' What is it ? ' I asked.
' My life and adventures,' he answered. ' It is not a
thing,' he answered, ' that can be published during my
lifetime, but you may have it if you like. There, do whatever you please with it.' In taking the bag, and thanking
him most warmly, I added, ' This will make a nice legacy
for my little Tom, who shall astonish the latter days of

the nineteenth century with it.'"[1]   Shortly after, Moore
for the last time bade his friend farewell, taking with him
from Madame Guiccioli, who did the honours of the
house, an introduction to her brother, Count Gamba, at
Rome. " Theresa Guiccioli," says Castelar, " appears like
a star on the stormy horizon of the poet's life." A young
Romagnese, the daughter of a nobleman of Ravenna, of
good descent but limited means, she had been educated
in a convent, and married in her nineteenth year to a
rich widower of sixty, in early life a friend of Alfieri,
and noted as the patron of the National Theatre. This
beautiful blonde, of pleasing manners, graceful presence,
and a strong vein of sentiment, fostered by the reading of
Chateaubriand, met Byron for the first time casually when
she came in her bridal dress to one of the Albrizzi re-
unions; but she was only introduced to him early in the
April of the following year, at the house of the Countess
Benzoni. " Suddenly the young Italian found herself
inspired with a passion of which till that moment her
mind could not have formed the least idea ; she had
thought of love but as an amusement, and now became its
slave." Byron, on the other hand, gave what remained
of a heart, never alienated from her by any other mistress.
Till the middle of the month they met every day ; and
when the husband took her back to Ravenna she des-

[1] In December, 1820, Byron sent several more sheets of memo-
randa from Ravenna, and in the following year suggested an
arrangement by which Murray paid over to Moore, who was then
in difficulties, 2000*l.* for the right of publishing the whole, under
the condition, among others, that Lady Byron should see them,
and have the right of reply to anything that might seem to her
objectionable. She on her part declined to have anything to do
with them. When the Memoirs were destroyed, Moore paid back
the 2000*l.*, but obtained four thousand guineas for editing the
*Life and Correspondence.*

patched to her idol a series of impassioned letters, declaring
her resolution to mould her life in accordance with his
wishes. Towards the end of May she had prepared her
relatives to receive Byron as a visitor. He started in
answer to the summons, writing on his way the beautiful
stanzas to the Po, beginning—

> River that rollest by the ancient walls
> Where dwells the lady of my love.

Again passing through Ferrara, and visiting Bologna, he
left the latter on the 8th, and on his arrival at his
destination found the Countess dangerously ill; but his
presence, and the attentions of the famous Venetian
doctor, Aglietti, who was sent for by his advice, restored
her. The Count seems to have been proud of his guest.
" I can't make him out at all," Byron writes ; " he visits
me frequently, and takes me out (like Whittington the
Lord Mayor) in a coach and six horses. The fact appears
to be, that he is completely governed by her—and, for that
matter, so am I." Later he speaks of having got his
horses from Venice, and riding or driving daily in the
scenery reproduced in the third canto of *Don Juan* :—

> Sweet hour of twilight ! in the solitude
> Of the pine forest, and the silent shore
> Which bounds Ravenna's immemorial wood.

On Theresa's recovery, in dread of a possible separation
he proposed to fly with her to America, to the Alps, to
" some unsuspected isle in the far seas ;" and she suggested
the idea of feigning death, like Juliet, and rising from the
tomb. Neither expedient was called for. When the
Count went to Bologna, in August, with his wife, Lord
Byron was allowed to follow ; and—after consoling
himself during an excursion which the married pair made

to their estate, by hovering about her empty rooms and
writing in her books—he established himself, on the
Count's return to his headquarters, with her and Allegra at
Bologna.  Meanwhile, Byron had written *The Prophecy of
Dante*, and in August the prose letter, *To the Editor of
the British Review*, on the charge of bribery in *Don Juan*.
Than this inimitable epistle no more laughter-compelling
composition exists.  About the same time, we hear of his
leaving the theatre in a convulsion of tears, occasioned
by the representation of Alfieri's *Mirra*.

He left Bologna with the Countess on the 15th of
September, when they visited the Euganean hills and
Arqua, and wrote their names together in the Pilgrim's
Book.  On arriving at Venice, the physicians recom-
mending Madame Guiccioli to country air, they settled,
still by her husband's consent, for the autumn at La
Mira, where Moore and others found them domesticated.
At the beginning of November the poet was prostrated
by an attack of tertian fever.  In some of his hours of
delirium he dictated to his careful nurses, Fletcher and
the Countess, a number of verses, which she assures us
were correct and sensible.  He attributes his restoration
to cold water and the absence of doctors ; but, ere his
complete recovery, Count Guiccioli had suddenly appeared
on the scene, and run away with his own wife.  The
lovers had for a time not only to acquiesce in the separation, but to agree to cease their correspondence.  In
December, Byron in a fit of spleen had packed up his
belongings, with a view to return to England.  "He was,"
we are told, "ready dressed for the journey, his boxes on
board the gondola, his gloves and cap on, and even his
little cane in his hand, when my lord declares that if it
should strike one—which it did—before everything was

in order, he would not go that day.   It is evident he had
not the heart to go." Next day he heard that Madame
Guiccioli was again seriously ill, received and accepted
the renewed invitation which bound him to her and to
the south.   He left Venice for the last time almost by
stealth, rushed along the familiar roads, and was welcomed
at Ravenna.

# CHAPTER VIII.

## 1820—1821.

BYRON'S life at Ravenna was during the first months comparatively calm ; nevertheless, he mingled in society, took part in the Carnival, and was received at the parties of the Legate. " I may stay," he writes in January, 1820, " a day—a week—a year—all my life." Meanwhile, he imported his movables from Venice, hired a suite of rooms in the Guiccioli palace, executed his marvellously close translation of Pulci's *Morgante Maggiore*, wrote his version of the story of *Francesca of Rimini*, and received visits from his old friend Bankes and from Sir Humphrey Davy. At this time he was accustomed to ride about armed to the teeth, apprehending a possible attack from assassins on the part of Count Guiccioli. In April his letters refer to the insurrectionary movements then beginning against the Holy Alliance. " We are on the verge of a row here. Last night they have over-written all the city walls with ' Up with the Republic ! ' and ' Death to the Pope ! ' The police have been searching for the subscribers, but have caught none as yet. The other day they confiscated the whole translation of the fourth canto of *Childe Harold*, and have prosecuted the translator." In July a Papal decree of separation between

the Countess and her husband was obtained, on condition
of the latter paying from his large income a pittance to the
lady of 200*l.* a year, and her undertaking to live in her
father's house—an engagement which was, first in the
spirit, and subsequently in the letter, violated. For a
time, however, she retired to a villa about fifteen miles
from Ravenna, where she was visited by Byron at comparatively rare intervals. By the end of July he had
finished *Marino Faliero*, and ere the close of the year the
fifth canto of *Don Juan*. In September he says to
Murray, " I am in a fierce humour at not having Scott's
*Monastery*. No more Keats,[1] I entreat. There is no
bearing the drivelling idiotism of the manikin. I don't
feel inclined to care further about *Don Juan*. What do
you think a very pretty Italian lady said to me the other
day, when I remarked that 'it would live longer than
*Childe Harold'?* 'Ah! but I would rather have the
fame of *Childe Harold* for three years than an immortality
of *D. J.*'" This is to-day the common female judgment ;
it is known to have been La Guiccioli's, as well as Mrs.
Leigh's, and by their joint persuasion Byron was for a
season induced to lay aside "that horrid, wearisome
Don." About this time he wrote the memorable reply to
the remarks on that poem in *Blackwood's Magazine*, where
he enters on a defence of his life, attacks the Lakers, and
champions Pope against the new school of poetry, lament-
ing that his own practice did not square with his precept ;

[1] In a note on a similar passage, bearing the date November
12, 1821, he, however, confesses :—" My indignation at Mr. Keats'
depreciation of Pope has hardly permitted me to do justice to his
own genius, which malgré all the fantastic fopperies of his style
was undoubtedly of great promise. His fragment of Hyperion
seems actually inspired by the Titans, and is as sublime as
Æschylus. He is a loss to our literature."

and adding, " We are all wrong, except Rogers, Crabbe,
and Campbell."

In November he refers to reports of his letters being
opened by the Austrian officials, and the unpleasant things
the Huns, as he calls them, are likely to find therein.
Early in the next month he tells Moore that the com-
mandant of their troops, a brave officer, but obnoxious to
the people, had been found lying at his door, with five
slugs in him, and, bleeding inwardly, had died in the
palace, where he had been brought to be nursed.

This incident is versified in *Don Juan*, v. 33—39,
with anatomical minuteness of detail.   After trying in
vain to wrench an answer out of death, the poet ends in
his accustomed strain—

> But it was all a mystery.   Here we are,
> And there we go :—but *where?*   Five bits of lead—
> Or three, or two, or one—send very far!

Assassination has sometimes been the prelude to revolution, but it may be questioned if it has ever promoted
the cause of liberty.   Most frequently it has served as a
pretext for reaction, or a red signal.   In this instance
—as afterwards in 1848—overt acts of violence made the
powers of despotism more alert, and conduced with the
half-hearted action of their adversaries to the suppression
of the rising of 1820-21.   Byron's sympathy with the
movement seems to have been stimulated by his new
associations.   Theresa's brother, Count Pietro, an enthusiastic young soldier, having returned from Rome and
Naples, surmounting a prejudice not wholly unnatural,
became attached to him, and they entered into a partner-
ship in behalf of what—adopting a phrase often flaunted
in opposite camps—they called constitutional principles.
Finally the poet so committed himself to the party of

insurrection that, though his nationality secured him from
direct attack, his movements were necessarily affected
by the fiasco. In July the Gambas were banished from
the Romagna, Pietro being actually carried by force
over the frontier; and, according to the articles of her
separation, the Countess had to follow them to Florence.
Byron lingered for some months, partly from a spirit of
defiance, and partly from his affection towards a place
where he had enlisted the regards of numerous beneficia-
ries. The Gambas were for some time bent on migrating
to Switzerland; but the poet, after first acquiescing,
subsequently conceived a violent repugnance to the idea,
and early in August wrote to Shelley, earnestly requesting
his presence, aid, and counsel. Shelley at once complied,
and, entering into a correspondence with Madame Guiccioli, succeeded in inducing her relatives to abandon their
transmontane plans, and agree to take up their headquarters at Pisa. This incident gave rise to a series of
interesting letters, in which the younger poet gives a
vivid and generous account of the surroundings and condition of his friend. On the 2nd of August he writes
from Ravenna :—"I arrived last night at ten o'clock, and
sat up talking with Lord B. till five this morning. He
was delighted to see me. He has, in fact, completely
recovered his health, and lives a life totally the reverse
of that which he led at Venice. . . . . Poor fellow ! he
is now quite well, and immersed in politics and literature.
We talked a great deal of poetry and such matters last
night, and, as usual, differed, I think, more than ever.
He affects to patronize a system of criticism fit only for
the production of mediocrity; and, although all his finer
poems and passages have been produced in defiance of
this system, yet I recognize the pernicious effects of it in

the *Doge of Venice.*" Again, on the 15th : " Lord B.
is greatly improved in every respect—in genius, in
temper, in moral views, in health, and happiness. His
connexion with La Guiccioli has been an inestimable
benefit to him. He lives in considerable splendour, but
within his income, which is now about 4000*l.* a year,
1000*l.* of which he devotes to purposes of charity.
Switzerland is little fitted for him ; the gossip and
the cabals of those Anglicised coteries would torment
him, as they did before. Ravenna is a miserable place.
He would in every respect be better among the Tuscans.
He has read to me one of the unpublished cantos of
*Don Juan.* It sets him not only above, but far above,
all the poets of the day. Every word has the stamp of
immortality. . . . . I have spoken to him of Hunt,
but not with a direct view of demanding a contribution.
I am sure, if I asked, it would not be refused ; yet there
is something in me that makes it impossible. Lord B.
and I are excellent friends ; and were I reduced to poverty,
or were I a writer who had no claim to a higher position
than I possess, I would freely ask him any favour. Such
is not now the case." Later, after stating that Byron
had decided upon Tuscany, he says, in reference to La
Guiccioli, " At the conclusion of a letter, full of all the
fine things she says she has heard of me, is this request,
which I transcribe :—' Signore, la vostra bontà mi fa ardita
di chiedervi un favore, me lo accordarete voi ? *Non
partite da Ravenna senza milord.*' Of course, being now
by all the laws of knighthood captive to a lady's request, I shall only be at liberty on my parole until Lord
Byron is settled at Pisa."

Shelley took his leave, after a visit of ten days' duration, about the 17th or 18th of April. In a letter, dated

August 26, he mentions having secured for his lordship
the Palazzo Lanfranchi, an old spacious building on the
Lung' Arno, once the family residence of the destroyers
of Ugolino, and still said to be haunted by their ghosts.
Towards the close of October, he says they have been ex-
pecting him any day these six weeks. Byron, however, did
not leave till the morning of the 29th.  On his road, there
occurred at Imola the accidental meeting with Lord Clare.
Clare—who on this occasion merely crossed his friend's
path on his way to Rome—at a later date came on purpose
from Geneva before returning to England to visit the
poet, who, then at Leghorn, recorded in a letter to Moore
his sense of this proof of old affection undecayed.  At
Bologna—his next stage—he met Rogers by appointment,
and the latter has preserved his memory of the event in
well-known lines.  Together they revisited Florence and
its galleries, where they were distracted by the crowds of
sight-seeing visitors.  Byron must have reached Pisa
not later than the 2nd of November (1821), for his first
letter from there bears the date of the 3rd.

The later months of the poet's life at Ravenna were
marked by intense literary activity.  Over a great part
of the year was spread the controversy with Bowles
about Pope, i.e. between the extremes of Art against
Nature, and Nature against Art.  It was a controversy
for the most part free from personal animus, and on Byron's
part the genuine expression of a reaction against a reaction.  To this year belong the greater number of the
poet's Historical Dramas.  What was said of these at the
time by Jeffrey, Heber, and others, was said with justice;
it is seldom that the criticism of our day finds so
little to reverse in that of sixty years ago.

The author, having shown himself capable of being

pathetic, sarcastic, sentimental, comical, and sublime, we
would be tempted to think that he had written these plays
to show, what no one before suspected, that he could also
be dull, were it not for his own exorbitant estimation
of them.  Lord Byron had few of the powers of a great
dramatist; he had little architectural imagination, or
capacity to conceive and build up a whole.  His works
are mainly masses of fine, splendid, or humorous writing,
heaped together; the parts are seldom forged into one, or
connected by any indissoluble link.  His so-called Dramas
are only poems divided into chapters.  Further, he had
little of what Mr. Ruskin calls Penetrative Imagination.
So it has been plausibly said that he made his men after
his own image, his women after his own heart.  The
former are, indeed, rather types of what he wished to be
than what he was.  They are better, and worse, than
himself.  They have stronger wills, more definite purposes, but less genial and less versatile natures.  But
it remains true, that when he tried to represent a character
totally different from himself, the result is either un-
real or uninteresting.  *Marino Faliero*, begun April,
finished July, 1820, and prefixed by a humorous dedication to Goethe—which was, however, suppressed—was
brought on the stage of Drury Lane Theatre early in
1821, badly mangled, appointed, and acted—and damned.

Byron seems to have been sincere in saying he did
not intend any of his plays to be represented.  We are
more inclined to accuse him of self-deception when he
asserts that he did not mean them to be popular; but he
took sure means to prevent them from being so.  *Marino
Faliero*, in particular, was pronounced by Dr. John
Watkins—old Grobius himself—"to be the dullest of
dull plays;" and even the warmest admirers of the poet

had to confess that the style was cumbrous. The story may be true, but it is none the less unnatural. The characters are comparatively commonplace, the women especially being mere shadows ; the motion is slow ; and the inevitable passages of fine writing are, as the extolled soliloquy of Lioni, rather rhetorical than imaginative. The speeches of the Doge are solemn, but prolix, if not ostentatious, and—perhaps the vital defect—his cause fails to enlist our sympathies.    Artistically, this play was Byron's most elaborate attempt to revive the unities and other restrictions of the severe style, which, when he wrote, had been "vanquished in literature."    " I am persuaded," he writes in the preface, " that a great tragedy is not to be produced by following the old dramatists, who are full of faults, but by producing regular dramas like the Greeks." He forgets that the statement in the mouth of a Greek dramatist that his play was not intended for the stage, would have been a confession of failure ; and that Aristotle had admitted that even the Deity could not make the Past present.    The ethical motives of Faliero are, first, the cry for vengeance—the feeling of affronted or unsatiated pride—that runs through so much of the author's writing, and second, the enthusiasm for public ends, which was beginning to possess him.    The following lines have been pointed out as embodying some of Byron's spirit of protest against the mere selfish " greasy domesticity " of the Georgian era :—

I. BER.                    Such ties are not
        For those who are called to the high destinies
        Which purify corrupted commonwealths :
        We must forget all feelings save the one,
        We must resign all passions save our purpose,
        We must behold no object save our country,
        And only look on death as beautiful

> So that the sacrifice ascend to heaven,
> And draw down freedom on her evermore.
> CAL.    But if we fail— ?
> I. BER.                    They never fail who die
> In a great cause : the block may soak their gore ;
> Their heads may sodden in the sun ; their limbs
> Be strung to city gates and castle walls,
> But still their spirit walks abroad.

—a passage which, after his wont, he spoils by platitudes about the precisian Brutus, who certainly did not give Rome liberty.

Byron's other Venetian Drama, the *Two Foscari*, composed at Ravenna, between the 11th of June and the 10th of July, 1821, and published in the following December, is another record of the same failure and the same mortification, due to the same causes. In this play, as Jeffrey points out, the preservation of the unities had a still more disastrous effect. The author's determination to avoid rant did not hinder his frequently adopting an inflated style ; while professing to follow the ancient rules, he forgets the warning of Horace so far as to permit the groans of the tortured Foscari to be heard on the stage. The declamations of Marina produce no effect on the action, and the vindictiveness of Loridano, though effectively pointed in the closing words, "He has paid me," is not rendered interesting, either by a well established injury, or by any trace of Iago's subtle genius.

In the same volume appeared *Sardanapalus*, written in the previous May, and dedicated to Goethe. In this play, which marks the author's last reversion to the East, we are more arrested by the majesty of the theme—

> Thirteen hundred years
> Of empire ending like a shepherd's tale,—

by the grandeur of some of the passages, and by the

development of the chief character, made more vivid by its being distinctly autobiographical. Sardanapalus himself is Harold, raised "high on a throne," and rousing himself at the close from a life of effeminate lethargy. Myrrha has been often identified with La Guiccioli, and the hero's relation to his Queen Zarina compared with that of the poet to his wife; but in his portrait of the former the author's defective capacity to represent national character is manifest: Myrrha is only another Gulnare, Medora, or Zuleika. In the domestic play of *Werner*—completed at Pisa in January, 1822, and published in November, there is no merit either of plan or execution; for the plot is taken, with little change, from "The German's Tale," written by Harriet Lee, and the treatment is throughout prosaic. Byron was never a master of blank verse; but *Werner*, his sole success on the modern British stage, is written in a style fairly parodied by Campbell, when he cut part of the author's preface into lines, and pronounced them as good as any in the play.

The *Deformed Transformed*, another adaptation, suggested by a forgotten novel called *The Three Brothers*, with reminiscences of *Faust*, and possibly of Scott's *Black Dwarf*, was begun at Pisa in 1821, but not published till January, 1824. This fragment owes its interest to the bitter infusion of personal feeling in the first scene, and its occasional charm to the march of some of the lines, especially those describing the Bourbon's advance on Rome; but the effect of the magical element is killed by previous parallels, while the story is chaotic and absurd. The *Deformed Transformed* bears somewhat the same relation to *Manfred* as *Heaven and Earth*—an occasionally graphic dream of the world before the Deluge, written October, 1821, and

L

issued about the same time as Moore's *Loves of the Angels*,
on a similar theme—does to *Cain*. The last named, begun
in July, and finished at Ravenna in September, is the
author's highest contribution to the metaphysical poetry
of the century. In *Cain* Byron grapples with the
perplexities of a belief which he never either accepted or
rejected, and with the yet deeper problems of life and
death, of good and ill. In dealing with these his position
is not that of one justifying the ways of God to man—
though he somewhat disingenuously appeals to Milton in
his defence—nor that of the definite antagonism of *Queen
Mab*. The distinction in this respect between Byron and
Shelley cannot be over-emphasized. The latter had a firm
faith other than that commonly called Christian. The
former was, in the proper sense of the word, a sceptic, beset
with doubts, and seeking for a solution which he never
found, shifting in his expression of them with every change
of a fickle and inconsistent temperament. The atmosphere
of *Cain* is almost wholly negative ; for under the guise of
a drama, which is mainly a dialogue between two halves
of his mind, the author appears to sweep aside with
something approaching to disdain the answers of a blindly
accepted tradition, or of a superficial optimism, e.g.—

> CAIN. Then my father's God did well
>     When he prohibited the fatal tree.
> LUCIFER. But had done better in not planting it.

Again, a kid, after suffering agonies from the sting of a
reptile, is restored by antidotes—

> Behold, my son! said Adam, how from evil
> Springs good!
> LUCIFER.         What didst thou answer ?
> CAIN.                 Nothing ; for
> He is my father ; but I thought, that 'twere

> A better portion for the animal
> Never to have been stung at all.

This rebellious nature naturally yields to the arguments
of Lucifer, a spirit in which much of the grandeur of
Milton's Satan is added to the subtlety of Mephistopheles.
In the first scene Cain is introduced, rebelling against
toils imposed on him by an offence committed before
he was born,—"I sought not to be born"—the answer, that toil is a good, being precluded by its authoritative representation as a punishment; in which mood
he is confirmed by the entrance and reasonings of the
Tempter, who identifies the Deity with Seva the De-
stroyer, hints at the dreadful visitation of the yet un-
tasted death; when Adah, entering, takes him at first
for an angel, and then recognizes him as a fiend. Her
invocation to Eve, and comparison of the "heedless,
harmless, wantonness of bliss" in Eden, to the later lot
of those girt about with demons from whose fascination
they cannot fly, is one of the most striking in the drama;
as is the line put into the mouth of the poet's most
beautiful female character, to show that God cannot be
alone,—

> What else can joy be, but diffusing joy?

Her subsequent contrast of Lucifer with the other
angels is more after the style of Shelley than anything
else in Byron—

> As the silent sunny moon,
> All light, they look upon us. But thou seemst
> Like an ethereal night, where long white clouds
> Streak the deep purple, and unnumber'd stars
> Spangle the wonderful mysterious vault
> With things that look as if they would be suns—
> So beautiful, unnumber'd and endearing;

> Not dazzling, and yet drawing us to them,
> They fill my eyes with tears, and so dost thou.

The flight with Lucifer, in the second act, in the abyss
of space and through the Hades of "uncreated night,"
with the vision of long-wrecked worlds, and the "inter-
minable gloomy realms

> Of swimming shadows and enormous shapes,

—suggested, as the author tells us, by the reading of
Cuvier—leaves us with impressions of grandeur and desolation which no other passages of English poetry can
convey.   Lord Byron has elsewhere exhibited more versatility of fancy and richness of illustration, but nowhere
else has he so nearly " struck the stars."   From constellation to constellation the pair speed on, cleaving the
blue with mighty wings, but finding in all a blank, like
that in Richter's wonderful dream.   The result on the
mind of Cain is summed in the lines on the fatal tree,—

> It was a lying tree—for we *know* nothing;
> At least, it *promised knowledge* at the price
> Of death—but *knowledge* still; but what *knows* man?

A more modern poet answers, after beating at the same
iron gates, " Behold, we know not anything."   The most
beautiful remaining passage is Cain's reply to the question—what is more beautiful to him than all that he
has seen in the " unimaginable ether"?—

> My sister Adah.—All the stars of heaven,
> The deep blue noon of night, lit by an orb
> Which looks a spirit, or a spirit's world—
> The hues of twilight—the sun's gorgeous coming—
> His setting indescribable, which fills
> My eyes with pleasant tears as I behold
> Him sink, and feel my heart flow softly with him
> Along that western paradise of clouds—

> The forest shade—the green bough—the bird's voice —
> The vesper bird's, which seems to sing of love,
> And mingles with the song of cherubim,
> As the day closes over Eden's walls :—
> All these are nothing, to my eyes and heart,
> Like Adah's face.

Lucifer's speech at the close of the act is perhaps too Miltonic to be absolutely original. Returning to earth, we have a pastoral, of which Sir Egerton Brydges justly and sufficiently remarks, "The censorious may say what they will, but there are speeches in the mouth of Cain and Adah, especially regarding their child, which nothing in English poetry but the 'wood-notes wild' of Shakespeare, ever equalled." Her cry, as Cain seems to threaten the infant, followed by the picture of his bloom and joy, is a touch of perfect pathos. Then comes the interview with the pious Abel, who is amazed at the lurid light in the eyes of his brother, with the spheres "singing in thunder round " him—the two sacrifices, the murder, the shriek of Zillah —

> Father ! Eve !
> Adah ! Come hither !  Death is in the world ;

Cain's rallying from stupor—

> I am awake at last—a dreary dream
> Had madden'd me,—but he shall never wake :

the curse of Eve ; and the close—μεῖζον ἢ κατὰ δάκρυα—

> CAIN.              Leave me.
> ADAH.                  Why all have left thee.
> CAIN. And wherefore lingerest thou ?  Dost thou not fear ?
> ADAH.                  I fear
> Nothing, except to leave thee.
> \*        \*        \*        \*        \*
> CAIN. Eastward from Eden will we take our way.

ADAH.  Leave! thou shalt be my guide; and may our God
          Be thine! Now let us carry forth our children.
CAIN.  And *he* who lieth there was childless.  I
          Have dried the fountain of a gentle race.
          O Abel!
ADAH.              Peace be with him.
CAIN.                                But with *me*!

*Cain,* between which and the *Cenci* lies the award of
the greatest single performance in dramatic shape of our
century, raised a storm.  It was published, with *Sardanapalus* and *The Two Foscari* in December, 1821, and
the critics soon gave evidence of the truth of Elze's
remark—" In England freedom of action is cramped by
the want of freedom of thought.  The converse is the case
with us Germans ; freedom of thought is restricted by the
want of freedom in action.  To us this scepticism presents
nothing in the least fearful."  But with us it appeared as
if a literary Guy Fawkes had been detected in the act
of blowing up half the cathedrals and all the chapels
of the country.  The rage of insular orthodoxy was in
proportion to its impotence.  Every scribbler with a
cassock denounced the book and its author, though few
attempted to answer him.  The hubbub was such that
Byron wrote to Murray, authorizing him to disclaim all
responsibility, and offering to refund the payment he had
received.  " Say that both you and Mr. Gifford remon-
strated.  I will come to England to stand trial.  ' Me me
adsum qui feci,' "—and much to the same effect.  The book
was pirated ; and on the publisher's application to have
an injunction, Lord Eldon refused to grant it.  The
majority of the minor reviewers became hysterical, and
Dr. Watkins, amid much almost inarticulate raving, said
that Sir Walter Scott, who had gratefully accepted
the dedication, would go down to posterity with the

brand of *Cain* upon his brow. Several even of the higher critics took fright. Jeffrey, while protesting his appreciation of the literary merits of the work, lamented its tendency to unsettle faith. Mr. Campbell talked of its "frightful audacity." Bishop Heber wrote at great length to prove that its spirit was more dangerous than that of *Paradise Lost*—and succeeded. The *Quarterly* began to cool towards the author. Moore wrote to him, that Cain was "wonderful, terrible, never to be forgotten," but "dreaded and deprecated" the influence of Shelley. Byron showed the letter to Shelley, who wrote to a common friend to assure Mr. Moore that he had not the smallest influence over his lordship in matters of religion, and only wished he had, as he would "employ it to eradicate from his great mind the delusions of Christianity, which seem perpetually to recur, and to lie in ambush for the hours of sickness and distress." Shelley elsewhere writes : "What think you of Lord B.'s last volume? In my opinion it contains finer poetry than has appeared in England since *Paradise Lost*. Cain is apocalyptic ; it is a revelation not before communicated to man." In the same strain, Scott says of the author of the "grand and tremendous drama :" "He has certainly matched Milton on his own ground." The worst effect of those attacks appears in the shifts to which Byron resorted to explain himself,—to be imputed, however, not to cowardice, but to his wavering habit of mind. Great writers in our country have frequently stirred difficult questions in religion and life, and then seemed to be half scared, like Rouget de Lisle, by the reverberation of their own voices. Shelley almost alone was always ready to declare, "I meant what I said, and stand to it."

Byron having, with or without design, arraigned some
of the Thirty-Nine Articles of his countrymen, proceeded in
the following month (October 1821) to commit an outrage,
yet more keenly resented, on the memory of their sainted
king, the pattern of private virtue and public vice, George
III. The perpetration of this occurred in the course of
the last of his numerous literary duels, of which it was
the close. That Mr. Southey was a well-meaning and
independent man of letters, there can be no doubt. It
does not require the conclusive testimony of the esteem
of Savage Landor to compel our respect for the author of
the *Life of Nelson*, and the open-handed friend of Coleridge ; nor is it any disparagement that, with the last-
named and with Wordsworth, he in middle life changed
his political and other opinions. But in his dealings with
Lord Byron, Southey had " eaten of the insane root." He
attacked a man of incomparably superior powers, for whom
his utter want of humour—save in its comparatively childish forms—made him a ludicrously unequal match, and
paid the penalty in being gibbeted in satires that will
endure with the language. The strife, which seems to
have begun on Byron's leaving England, rose to its height
when his lordship, in the humorous observations and
serious defence of his character against " the Remarks " in
Blackwood, 1819 (August), accused the Laureate of apo-
stasy, treason, and slander.

In 1821, when the latter published his *Vision of Judgment*—the most quaintly preposterous panegyric ever
penned—he prefixed to it a long explanatory note, in
the course of which he characterizes *Don Juan* as a " mon-
strous combination of horror and mockery, lewdness and
impiety," regrets that it has not been brought under the
lash of the law, salutes the writer as chief of the

Satanic school, inspired by the spirits of Moloch and
Belial, and refers to the remorse that will overtake him
on his death-bed. To which Byron, *inter alia:* "Mr.
Southey, with a cowardly ferocity, exults over the anticipated death-bed repentance of the objects of his dislike,
and indulges himself in a pleasant ' Vision of Judgment,' in
prose, as well as verse, full of impious impudence. What
Mr. Southey's sensations or ours may be in the awful moment of leaving this state of existence, neither he nor we
can pretend to decide. In common, I presume, with most
men of any reflection, *I* have not waited for a death-bed
to repent of many of my actions, notwithstanding the
' diabolical pride ' which this pitiful renegado in his ran-
cour would impute to those who scorn him." This dignified, though trenchant, rejoinder would have been un-
answerable ; but the writer goes on to charge the Laureate
with spreading calumnies. To this charge Southey, in
January, 1822, replies with "a direct and positive denial,"
and then proceeds to talk at large of the "whip and
branding iron," "slaves of sensuality," "stones from
slings," "Goliahs," "public panders," and what not, in the
manner of the brave days of old.

In February Byron, having seen this assault in the
*Courier*, writes off in needless heat, "I have got Southey's
pretended reply ; what remains to be done is to call him
out,"—and despatches a cartel of mortal defiance. Mr.
Douglas Kinnaird, through whom this was sent, judiciously
suppressed it, and the author's thirst for literary blood
was destined to remain unquenched. Meanwhile he had
written his own *Vision of Judgment.* This extraordinary
work, having been refused by both Murray and Longman,
appeared in 1822 in the pages of the *Liberal.* It passed
the bounds of British endurance ; and the publisher, Mr.

John Hunt, was prosecuted and fined for the publication.

Readers of our day will generally admit that the " gouty hexameters " of the original poem, which celebrates the apotheosis of King George in heaven, are much more blasphemous than the *ottava rima* of the travesty, which professes to narrate the difficulties of his getting there. Byron's *Vision of Judgment* is as unmistakably the first of parodies as the *Iliad* is the first of epics, or the *Pilgrim's Progress* the first of allegories. In execution it is almost perfect. *Don Juan* is in scope and magnitude a far wider work ; but no considerable series of stanzas in *Don Juan* are so free from serious artistic flaw. From first to last, every epithet hits the white ; every line that does not convulse with laughter stings or lashes. It rises to greatness by the fact that, underneath all its lambent buffoonery, it is aflame with righteous wrath. Nowhere in such space, save in some of the prose of Swift, is there in English so much scathing satire.

# CHAPTER IX.

## 1821—1823.

PISA—GENOA—DON JUAN.

BYRON, having arrived at Pisa with his troop of carriages, horses, dogs, fowls, monkeys, and servants, settled himself quietly in the Palazzo Lanfranchi for ten months, interrupted only by a sojourn of six weeks in the neighbourhood of Leghorn. His life in the old feudal building followed in the main the tenour of his life at Ravenna. He rose late, received visitors in the afternoons, played billiards, rode or practised with his pistols, in concert with Shelley, whom he refers to at this time as " the most companionable man under thirty " he had ever met. Both poets were good shots, but Byron the safest; for, though his hand often shook, he made allowance for the vibration, and never missed his mark. On one occasion he set up a slender cane, and at twenty paces divided it with his bullet. The early part of the evening he gave to a frugal meal and the society of La Guiccioli—now apparently, in defiance of the statute of limitations, established under the same roof—and then sat late over his verses. He was disposed to be more sociable than at Venice or Ravenna, and occasionally entertained strangers ; but his intimate acquaintanceship was confined to Captain Williams and his wife, and Shelley's cousin, Captain

Medwin. The latter used frequently to dine and sit with
his host till the morning, collecting materials for the *Conversations* which he afterwards gave to the world. The
value of these reminiscences is impaired by the fact of
their recording, as serious revelations, the absurd confidences in which the poet's humour for mystification was
wont to indulge. Another of the group, an Irishman,
called Taafe, is made, in his Lordship's correspondence of
the period, to cut a somewhat comical figure. The master-
passion of this worthy and genial fellow was to get a
publisher for a fair commentary on Dante, to which he
had firmly linked a very bad translation, and for about
six months Byron pesters Murray with constant appeals
to satisfy him ; e. g. November 16, "He must be gratified,
though the reviewers will make him suffer more tortures
than there are in his original." March 6, "He will
die if he is not published ; he will be damned if he
is ; but that he don't mind." March 8, "I make it
a point that he shall be in print; it will make the
man so exuberantly happy. He is such a good-natured
Christian that we must give him a shove through the
press. Besides, he has had another fall from his horse
into a ditch." Taafe, whose horsemanship was on a par
with his poetry, can hardly have been consulted as to
the form assumed by these apparently fruitless recom-
mendations, so characteristic of the writer's frequent
kindliness and constant love of mischief. About this
time Byron received a letter from Mr. Shepherd, a
gentleman in Somersetshire, referring to the death of
his wife, among whose papers he had found the record
of a touching, because evidently heart-felt, prayer for
the poet's reformation, conversion, and restored peace
of mind. To this letter he at once returned an answer,

marked by much of the fine feeling of his best moods.
Pisa, December 8 : " Sir, I have received your letter.   I
need not say that the extract which it contains has
affected me, because it would imply a want of all feeling
to have read it with indifference. . . . Your brief and
simple picture of the excellent person, whom I trust you
will again meet, cannot be contemplated without the
admiration due to her virtues and her pure and unpre-
tending piety.   I do not know that I ever met with
anything so unostentatiously beautiful.   Indisputably,
the firm believers in the Gospel have a great advantage
over all others—for this simple reason, that if true they
will have their reward hereafter ; and if there be no
hereafter, they can but be with the infidel in his eternal
sleep. . . . But a man's creed does not depend upon
*himself :* who can say, I *will* believe this, that, or the
other ? and least of all that which he least can comprehend. . . . I can assure you that not all the fame which
ever cheated humanity into higher notions of its own
importance, would ever weigh in my mind against the
pure and pious interest which a virtuous being may be
pleased to take in my behalf.   In this point of view I
would not exchange the prayer of the deceased in my
behalf for the united glory of Homer, Cæsar, and
Napoleon."

The letter to Lady Byron, which he afterwards
showed to Lady Blessington, must have borne about
the same date ; and we have a further indication of
his thoughts reverting homeward in an urgent request to
Murray—written on December 10th, Ada's sixth birthday—
to send his daughter's miniature.   After its arrival nothing
gave him greater pleasure than to be told of its strong
likeness to himself.   In the course of the same month an

event occurred which strangely illustrates the manners of
the place, and the character of the two poets. An unfortunate fanatic having taken it into his head to steal
the wafer-box out of a church at Lucca, and being
detected, was, in accordance with the ecclesiastical law
till lately maintained against sacrilege, condemned to
be burnt alive. Shelley, who believed that the sentence
would really be carried into effect, proposed to Byron that
they should gallop off together, and by aid of their
servants rescue by force the intended victim. Byron,
however, preferred in the first place, to rely on diplo-
macy ; some vigorous letters passed ; ultimately a representation, conveyed by Taafe to the English Ambassador,
led to a commutation of the sentence, and the man was
sent to the galleys.

The January of 1822 was marked by the addition to
the small circle of Captain E. J. Trelawny, the famous rover
and bold free-lance (now sole survivor of the remarkable
group), who accompanied Lord Byron to Greece, and has
recorded a variety of incidents of the last months of his
life. Trelawny, who appreciated Shelley with an intensity that is often apt to be exclusive, saw, or has reported, for the most part the weaker side of Byron. We
are constrained to accept as correct the conjecture that his
judgment was biassed by their rivalry in physical prowess,
and the political differences which afterwards developed
between them. Letters to his old correspondents—to
Scott about the *Waverleys*, to Murray about the Dramas,
and the *Vision of Judgment*, and *Cain*—make up almost
the sole record of the poet's pursuits during the five following months. On February 6th he sent, through Mr. Kinnaird, the challenge to Southey, of the suppression of which
he was not aware till May 17. The same letter contains a

IX.] AT PISA. 159

sheaf of the random cynicisms, as—" Cash is virtue,"
"Money is power; and when Socrates said he knew nothing,
he meant he had not a drachma "—by which he sharpened
the shafts of his assailants. A little later, on occasion of
the death of Lady Noel, he expresses himself with natural
bitterness on hearing that she had in her will recorded
a wish against his daughter Ada seeing his portrait. In
March he sat, along with La Guiccioli, to the sculptor
Bartolini. On the 24th, when the company were on one
of their riding excursions outside the town, a half-
drunken dragoon on horseback broke through them, and
by accident or design knocked Shelley from his seat.
Byron, pursuing him along the Lung' Arno, called for
his name, and, taking him for an officer, flung his glove.
The sound of the fray brought the servants of the
Lanfranchi to the door; and one of them, it was presumed—
though in the scuffle everything remained uncertain—
seriously wounded the dragoon in the side. An investi-
gation ensued, as the result of which the Gambas were
ultimately exiled from Tuscany, and the party of friends
was practically broken up. Shelley and his wife, with
the Williamses and Trelawny, soon after settled at the
Villa Magni at Lerici in the Gulf of Spezia. Byron,
with the Countess and her brother, established themselves
in the Villa Rossa at Monte Nero, a suburb of Leghorn,
from which port at this date the remains of Allegra were
conveyed to England.

Among the incidents of this residence were, the
homage paid to the poet by a party of Americans; the
painting of his portrait and that of La Guiccioli by their
compatriot, West, who has left a pleasing account of his
visits; Byron's letter making inquiry about the country of Bolivar (where it was his fancy to settle);

and another of those disturbances by which he seemed
destined to be harassed. One of his servants—among
whom were unruly spirits, apparently selected with a
kind of *Corsair* bravado,—had made an assault on Count
Pietro, wounding him in the face. This outburst,
though followed by tears and penitence, confirmed the
impression of the Tuscan police that the whole company
were dangerous, and made the Government press for their
departure. In the midst of the uproar, there suddenly
appeared at the villa Mr. Leigh Hunt, with his wife and
six children. They had taken passage to Genoa, where
they were received by Trelawny, in command of the
"Bolivar"—a yacht constructed in that port for Lord
Byron, simultaneously with the "Don Juan" for Shelley.
The latter, on hearing of the arrival of his friends, came
to meet them at Leghorn, and went with them to Pisa.
Early in July they were all established on the Lung'
Arno, having assigned to them the ground floor of the
palazzo.

We have now to deal briefly—amid conflicting assevera-
tions it is hard to deal fairly—with the last of the vexa-
tiously controverted episodes which need perplex our
narrative. Byron, in wishing Moore from Ravenna a merry
Christmas for 1820, proposes that they shall embark together in a newspaper, "with some improvement on
the plan of the present scoundrels," "to give the age
some new lights on policy, poesy, biography, criticism,
morality, theology," &c. Moore absolutely refusing to
entertain the idea, Hunt's name was brought forward in
connexion with it, during the visit of Shelley. Shortly
after the return of the latter to Pisa, he writes (August 26)
to Hunt, stating that Byron was anxious to start a
periodical work, to be conducted in Italy, and had pro-

posed that they should both go shares in the concern, on which follow some suggestions of difficulties about money. Nevertheless, in August, 1821, he presses Hunt to come.    Moore, on the other hand, strongly remonstrates against the project.    " I heard some days ago that Leigh Hunt was on his way to you with all his family ; and the idea seems to be that you and he and Shelley are to conspire together in the *Examiner*.    I deprecate such a plan with all my might.    Partnerships in fame, like those in trade, make the strongest party answer for the rest.    I tremble even for you with such a bankrupt Co.! You must stand alone."    Shelley—who had, in the meantime, given his bond to Byron for an advance of 200*l*. towards the expenses of his friends, besides assisting them himself to the utmost of his power—began, shortly before their arrival, to express grave doubts as to the success of the alliance.    His last published letter—written July 5th, 1822—after they had settled at Pisa, is full of forebodings.    On the 8th he set sail in the " Don Juan "—

> That fatal and perfidious bark,
> Built in th' eclipse, and rigg'd with curses dark,

and was overtaken by the storm in which he perished. Three days after, Trelawny rode to Pisa, and told Byron of his fears, when the poet's lips quivered, and his voice faltered.    On the 22nd of July the bodies of Shelley, Williams, and Vivian, were cast ashore.    On the 16th August, Hunt, Byron, and Trelawny were present at the  terribly  weird  cremation,  which  they  have  all described,  and  after  which  they  were  seized  with  a  fit of  the  hilarious  delirium  which  is  one  of  the  phases of  the  tension  of  grief.    Byron's  references  to  the  event are  expressions  less  of  the  loss  which  he  indubitably

M

felt, than of his indignation at the "world's wrong."
"Thus," he writes, "there is another man gone, about
whom the world was ill-naturedly and ignorantly and
brutally mistaken. It will, perhaps, do him justice now,
when he can be no better for it." Towards the end of
the same letter the spirit of his dead friend seems to
inspire the sentence—"With these things and these
fellows it is necessary, in the present clash of philosophy
and tyranny, to throw away the scabbard. I know it is
against fearful odds, but the battle must be fought."

Meanwhile, shortly after the new settlement at the
Lanfranchi, the preparations for issuing the *Liberal*,
edited by Leigh Hunt in Italy, and published by John
Hunt in London, progressed. The first number, which
appeared in September, was introduced, after a few words
of preface, by the *Vision of Judgment*, with the signature
Quevedo Redivivus, and adorned by Shelley's translation
of the "May-Day Night," in *Faust*. It contained besides, the *Letter to the Editor of my Grandmother's
Review*, an indifferent Florentine story, a German apo-
logue, and a gossiping account of Pisa, presumably by
Hunt. Three others followed, containing Byron's *Heaven
and Earth*, his translation of the *Morgante Maggiore*, and
*The Blues*—a very slight, if not silly, satire on literary
ladies ; some of Shelley's posthumous minor poems, among
them "I arise from dreams of thee," and a few of Hazlitt's
essays, including, however, none of his best. Leigh Hunt
himself wrote most of the rest, one of his contributions
being a palpable imitation of *Don Juan*, entitled the *Book
of Beginnings*, but he confesses that owing to his weak
health and low spirits at the time, none of these did
justice to his ability ; and the general manner of the
magazine being insufficiently vigorous to carry off the

frequent eccentricity of its matter, the prejudices against
it prevailed, and the enterprise came to an end.  Part-
ners in failing concerns are apt to dispute ; in this
instance the unpleasantness which arose at the time
rankled in the mind of the survivor, and gave rise
to his singularly tasteless and injudicious book—a performance which can be only in part condoned by the
fact of Hunt's afterwards expressing regret, and practically withdrawing it.  He represents himself throughout
as a much-injured man, lured to Italy by misrepresenta-
tions, that he might give the aid of his journalistic experience and undeniable talents to the advancement of a
mercenary enterprise, and that when it failed he was de-
spised, insulted, and rejected.   Byron, on the other hand,
declares, "The Hunts pressed me to engage in this work,
and in an evil hour I consented ; " and his subsequent
action in the matter, if not always gentle never unjust,
goes to verify his statements in the letters of the period.
" I am afraid," he writes from Genoa, Oct. 9, 1822,
" the journal is a bad business.  I have done all I can
for Leigh Hunt since he came here ; but it is almost useless.   His wife is ill, his six children not very tractable,
and in the affairs of this world he himself is a child."
Later he says to Murray, " You and your friends, by
your injudicious rudeness, cement a connexion which you
strove to prevent, and which, had the Hunts prospered,
would not in all probability have continued.  As it is . . .
I can't leave them among the breakers."   On February
20th we have, his last word on the subject, to the same
effect.

In the following sentences, Moore seems to give a
fair statement of the motives which led to the establishment of the unfortunate journal :—" The chief induce-

ments on the part of Lord Byron to this unworthy alliance
were, in the first place, a wish to second the kind views of
his friend Shelley in inviting Mr. Hunt to Italy; and in
the next, a desire to avail himself of the aid of one so
experienced as an editor in the favourite object he has so
long contemplated of a periodical work in which all the
offspring of his genius might be received as they sprung
to light." For the accomplishment of this purpose Mr.
Leigh Hunt was a singularly ill-chosen associate. A man
of Radical opinions on all matters, not only of religion but
of society—opinions which he acquired and held easily but
firmly—could never recognize the propriety of the claim
to deference which "the noble poet" was always too eager
to assert, and was inclined to take liberties which his
patron perhaps superciliously repelled. Mrs. Hunt does not
seem to have been a very judicious person. "Trelawny
here," said Byron jocularly, "has been speaking against
my morals." "It is the first time I ever heard of them,"
she replied. Mr. Hunt, by his own admission, had "peculiar notions on the subject of money." Byron, on his part,
was determined not to be "put upon," and doled out through
his steward stated allowances to Hunt, who says that only
" stern necessity and a large family" induced him to accept
them. Hunt's expression that the 200*l.* was, *in the first
instance*, a debt to Shelley, points to the conclusion that it
was remitted on that poet's death. Besides this, Byron
maintained the family till they left Genoa for Florence
in 1823, and defrayed up to that date all their expenses.
He gave his contributions to the *Liberal* gratis; and,
again by Hunt's own confession, left to him and his brother the profits of the proprietorship. According to Mr.
Galt " The whole extent of the pecuniary obligation
appears not to have exceeded 500*l.* ; but, little or great,

the manner in which it was recollected reflects no credit
either on the head or heart of the debtor."

Of the weaknesses on which the writer—bent on verifying
Pope's lines on Atossa—from his vantage in the ground-
floor, was enabled to dilate, many are but slightly magnified.
We are told for instance, in very many words, that Byron
clung to the privileges of his rank while wishing to seem
above them ; that he had a small library, and was a
one-sided critic ; that Bayle and Gibbon supplied him
with the learning he had left at school ; that, being a
good rider with a graceful seat, he liked to be told of it ;
that he showed letters he ought not to have shown ;
that he pretended to think worse of Wordsworth than
he did ; that he knew little of art or music, adored
Rossini, and called Rubens a dauber ; that, though he
wrote *Don Juan* under gin and water, he had not a
strong head, &c., &c. It is true, but not new. But
when Hunt proceeds to say that Byron had no sentiment ;
that La Guiccioli did not really care much about him ;
that he admired Gifford because he was a sycophant, and
Scott because he loved a lord ; that he had no heart for
anything except a feverish notoriety ; that he was a miser
from his birth, and had " as little regard for liberty as
Alfieri,"— it is new enough, but it is manifestly not true.
Hunt's book, which begins with a caricature on the frontispiece, and is inspired in the main by uncharitableness,
yet contains here and there gleams of a deeper insight
than we find in all the volumes of Moore—an insight,
which, in spite of his irritated egotism, is the mark of a
man with the instincts of a poet, with some cosmopolitan
sympathies, and a courage on occasion to avow them at
any risk. "Lord Byron," he says truly, "has been too
much admired by the English because he was sulky and

wilful, and reflected in his own person their love of
dictation and excitement.  They owe his memory a greater
regard, and would do it much greater honour if they
admired him for letting them know they were not so perfect a nation as they supposed themselves, and that
they might take as well as give lessons of humanity,
by a candid comparison of notes with civilization at
large."

In July, when at Leghorn, the Gambas received orders
to leave Tuscany; and on his return to Pisa, Byron, being
persecuted by the police, began to prepare for another
change.  After entertaining projects about Greece, America,
and Switzerland — Trelawny undertaking to have the
"Bolivar" conveyed over the Alps to the Lake of Geneva—
he decided on following his friends to Genoa.   He left in
September with La Guiccioli, passed by Lerici and Sestri,
and then for the ten remaining months of his Italian life
took up his quarters at Albaro, about a mile to the east of the
city, in the Villa Saluzzo, which Mrs. Shelley had procured
for him and his party.   She herself settled with the Hunts
—who travelled about the same time, at Byron's expense, but
in their own company—in the neighbouring Casa Negroto.
Not far off, Mr. Savage Landor was in possession of the
Casa Pallavicini, but there was little intercourse between
the three.   Landor and Byron, in many respects more
akin than any other two Englishmen of their age,
were always separated by an unhappy bar or intervening
mist.   The only family with whom the poet maintained
any degree of intimacy was that of the Earl of Blessington,
consisting of the Earl himself—a gouty old gentleman,
with stories about him of the past—the Countess, and
her sister, Miss Power, and the "cupidon déchaîné,"
the Anglo-French Count Alfred d'Orsay—who were to

ix.]       GENOA.       167

take part in stories of the future. In the spring of 1823,
Byron persuaded them to occupy the Villa Paradiso, and
was accustomed to accompany them frequently on horseback excursions along the coast to their favourite Nervi.
It has been said that Lady Blessington's *Conversations
with Lord Byron* are, as regards trustworthiness, on a par
with Landor's *Imaginary Conversations.* Let this be
so, they are still of interest on points of fact which
it must have been easier to record than to imagine.
However adorned, or the reverse, by the fancies of a
habitual novelist, they convey the impressions of a good-
humoured, lively, and fascinating woman, derived from
a more or less intimate association with the most brilliant
man of the age. Of his personal appearance—a matter
of which she was a good judge—we have the following : " One of Byron's eyes was larger than the other ;
his nose was rather thick, so he was best seen in
profile ; his mouth was splendid, and his scornful expression was real, not affected ; but a sweet smile
often broke through his melancholy. He was at this
time very pale and thin (which indicates the success
of his regimen of reduction since leaving Venice).
His hair was dark brown, here and there turning grey.
His voice was harmonious, clear and low. There is some
gaucherie in his walk, from his attempts to conceal his
lameness. Ada's portrait is like him, and he is pleased at
the likeness, but hoped she would not turn out to be clever—
at any events not poetical. He is fond of gossip, and apt
to speak slightingly of some of his friends, but is loyal to
others. His great defect is flippancy, and a total want of self-
possession." The narrator also dwells on his horror of inter-
viewers, by whom at this time he was even more than usually
beset. One visitor of the period ingenuously observes—

"Certain persons will be chagrined to hear that Byron's mode of life does not furnish the smallest food for calumny." Another says, "I never saw a countenance more composed and still—I might even add, more sweet and prepossessing. But his temper was easily ruffled and for a whole day; he could not endure the ringing of bells, bribed his neighbours to repress their noises, and failing, retaliated by surpassing them; he never forgave Colonel Carr for breaking one of his dog's ribs, though he generally forgave injuries without forgetting them. He had a bad opinion of the inertness of the Genoese; for whatever he himself did he did with a will—' toto se corpore miscuit,' and was wont to assume a sort of dictatorial tone—as if ' I have said it, and it must be so' were enough."

From these waifs and strays of gossip we return to a subject of deeper interest. The Countess of Blessington, with natural curiosity, was anxious to elicit from Byron some light on the mystery of his domestic affairs, and renewed the attempt previously made by Madame de Staël, to induce him to some movement towards a reconciliation with his wife. His reply to this overture was to show her a letter which he had written to Lady Byron from Pisa, but never forwarded, of the tone of which the following extracts must be a sufficient indication :—" I have to acknowledge the receipt of Ada's hair. . . . . I also thank you for the inscription of the date and name; and I will tell you why. I believe they are the only two or three words of your hand-writing in my possession, for your letters I returned, and except the two words—or rather the one word 'household' written twice—in an old account book, I have no other. Every day which keeps us asunder should, after so long a period, rather soften

our mutual feelings, which must always have one rallying-point as long as our child exists. We both made
a bitter mistake, but now it is over. I considered our
re-union as not impossible for more than a year
after the separation, but then I gave up the hope.
I am violent, but not malignant ; for only fresh provoca-
tions can awaken my resentment. Remember that if
you have injured me in aught, this forgiveness is something, and that if I have injured you, it is something
more still, if it be true, as moralists assert, that the most
offending are the least forgiving." "It is a strange business," says the Countess, about Lady Byron. "When
he was praising her mental and personal qualifications, I
asked him how all that he now said agreed with certain
sarcasms supposed to be a reference to her in his works.
He smiled, shook his head, and said, they were meant to
spite and vex her, when he was wounded and irritated at
her refusing to receive or answer his letters ; that he was
sorry he had written them, but might on similar pro-
vocations recur to the same vengeance." On another
occasion he said, "Lady B.'s first idea is what is due
to herself. I wish she thought a little more of what
is due to others. My besetting sin is a want of that self-
respect which she has in excess. When I have broken
out, on slight provocation, into one of my ungovernable
fits of rage, her calmness piqued and seemed to reproach
me ; it gave her an air of superiority that vexed and
increased my *mauvaise humeur*." To Lady Blessington
as to every one, he always spoke of Mrs. Leigh with the
same unwavering admiration, love, and respect.

"My first impressions were melancholy—my poor mother
gave them: but to my sister, who, incapable of wrong herself, suspected no wrong in others, I owe the little good of

which I can boast : and had I earlier known her it might
have influenced my destiny. Augusta was to me in the
hour of need a tower of strength. Her affection was my
last rallying-point, and is now the only bright spot that the
horizon of England offers to my view. She has given me
such good advice—and yet finding me incapable of following
it, loved and pitied me but the more because I was erring."
Similarly, in the height of his spleen, writes Leigh Hunt—
" I believe there did exist one person to whom he would
have been generous, if she pleased : perhaps was so. At
all events, he left her the bulk of his property, and always
spoke of her with the greatest esteem. This was his sister,
Mrs. Leigh. He told me she used to call him ' Baby
Byron.' It was easy to see that of the two persons she
had by far the greater judgment."

Byron having laid aside *Don Juan* for more than a
year, in deference to La Guiccioli, was permitted to
resume it again, in July, 1822, on a promise to observe
the proprieties. Cantos vi.—xi. were written at Pisa.
Cantos xii.—xvi. at Genoa, in 1823. These latter portions
of the poem were published by John Hunt. His other
works of the period are of minor consequence. The *Age
of Bronze* is a declamation, rather than a satire, directed
against the Convention of Cintra and the Congress of
Verona, especially Lord Londonderry's part in the
latter, only remarkable, from its advice to the Greeks,
to dread—

> The false friend worse than the infuriate foe ;

i. e. to prefer the claw of the Tartar savage to the paternal
hug of the great Bear—

> Better still toil for masters, than await,
> The slave of slaves, before a Russian gate.

In the *Island*—a tale of the mutiny of the "Bounty"—
he reverts to the manner and theme of his old romances,
finding a new scene in the Pacific for the exercise of
his fancy. In this piece his love of nautical adventure
reappears, and his idealization of primitive life, caught
from Rousseau and Chateaubriand. There is more
repose about this poem than in any of the author's other
compositions. In its pages the sea seems to plash about
rocks and caves that bask under a southern sun.
"'Byron, the sorcerer,' he can do with me what he
will," said old Dr. Parr, on reading it. As the swan-
song of the poet's sentimental verse, it has a pleasing
if not pathetic calm. During the last years in Italy he
planned an epic on the Conquest, and a play on the subject of Hannibal, neither of which was executed.

In the criticism of a famous work there is often little
left to do but to criticise the critics—to bring to a focus
the most salient things that have been said about it,
to eliminate the absurd from the sensible, the discrimi-
nating from the commonplace. *Don Juan*, more than any
of its precursors, *is* Byron, and it has been similarly
handled. The early cantos were ushered into the world
amid a chorus of mingled applause and execration. The
minor Reviews, representing middle-class respectability,
were generally vituperative, and the higher authorities divided in their judgments. The *British Magazine* said that
"his lordship had degraded his personal character by
the composition;" the *London*, that the poem was "a
satire on decency;" the *Edinburgh Monthly*, that it was
"a melancholy spectacle;" the *Eclectic*, that it was "an
outrage worthy of detestation." *Blackwood* declared
that the author was "brutally outraging all the best feelings of humanity." Moore characterizes it as "the most

painful display of the versatility of genius that has ever
been left for succeeding ages to wonder at or deplore."
Jeffrey found in the whole composition " a tendency to
destroy all belief in the reality of virtue ;" and Dr. John
Watkins classically named it " the Odyssey of Immorality."
" *Don Juan* will be read," wrote one critic, " as long as
satire, wit, mirth, and supreme excellence shall be esteemed
among men." " Stick to *Don Juan*," exhorted another;
" it is the only sincere thing you have written, and it will
live after all your *Harolds* have ceased to be 'a schoolgirl's
tale, the wonder of an hour.' It is the best of all your
works—the most spirited, the most straightforward, the
most interesting, the most poetical." " It is a work,"
said Goethe, " full of soul, bitterly savage in its misanthropy, exquisitely delicate in its tenderness." Shelley
confessed, " It fulfils in a certain degree what I have long
preached, the task of producing something wholly new and
relative to the age, and yet surpassingly beautiful." And
Sir Walter Scott, in the midst of a hearty panegyric : " It
has the variety of Shakespeare himself. Neither *Childe
Harold*, nor the most beautiful of Byron's earlier tales,
contain more exquisite poetry than is to be found scattered
through the cantos of *Don Juan*, amidst verses which
the author seems to have thrown from him with an effort
as spontaneous as that of a tree resigning its leaves."

One noticeable feature about these comments is their
sincerity : reviewing, however occasionally one-sided, had
not then sunk to be the mere register of adverse or friendly
cliques ; and, with all his anxiety for its verdict, Byron
never solicited the favour of any portion of the press.
Another is, the fact that the adverse critics missed their
mark. They had not learnt to say of a book of which they
disapproved, that it was weak or dull : in pronouncing

it to be vicious, they helped to promote its sale ; and the
most decried has been the most widely read of the author's
works.    Many of the readers of *Don Juan* have, it must
be confessed, been found among those least likely to admire
in it what is most admirable—who have been attracted by
the very excesses of buffoonery, violations of good taste, and
occasionally almost vulgar slang, which disfigure its pages.
Their patronage is, at the best, of no more value than that
of a mob gathered by a showy Shakespearian revival, and
it has laid the volume open to the charge of being adapted
"laudari ab illaudatis."    But the welcome of the work
in other quarters is as indubitably due to higher qualities.
In writing *Don Juan*, Byron attempted something that had
never been done before, and his genius so chimed with his
enterprise that it need never be done again.    " Down,"
cries M. Chasles, " with the imitators who did their best
to make his name ridiculous."    In commenting on their
failure, an excellent critic has explained the pre-established
fitness of the ottava rima—the first six lines of which
are a dance, and the concluding couplet a " breakdown "
—for the mock-heroic.    Byron's choice of this measure
may have been suggested by Whistlecraft; but he
had studied its cadence in Pulci, and the *Novelle
Galanti* of Casti, to whom he is indebted for other
features of his satire; and he added to what has
been well termed its characteristic jauntiness, by his
almost constant use of the double rhyme.    That the
ottava rima is out of place in consistently pathetic
poetry, may be seen from its obvious misuse in Keats's
*Pot of Basil.*  Many writers, from Frere to Moultrie, have
employed it successfully in burlesque or mere society
verse ; but Byron alone has employed it triumphantly, for
he has made it the vehicle of thoughts grave as well as

gay, of " black spirits and white, red spirits and grey," of
sparkling fancy, bitter sarcasm, and tender memories.
He has swept into the pages of his poem the experience
of thirty years of a life so crowded with vitality that our
sense of the plethora of power which it exhibits makes us
ready to condone its lapses. Byron, it has been said,
balances himself on a ladder like other acrobats ; but
alone, like the Japanese master of the art, he all the while
bears on his shoulders the weight of a man. Much of
*Don Juan* is as obnoxious to criticism in detail as his
earlier work ; it has every mark of being written in hot
haste. In the midst of the most serious passages (e. g. the
" Ave Maria ") we are checked in our course by bathos
or commonplace and thrown where the writer did not
mean to throw us : but the mocking spirit is so prevail-
ingly present that we are often left in doubt as to his
design, and what is in *Harold* an outrage is in this case
only a flaw. His command over the verse itself is almost
miraculous : he glides from extreme to extreme, from
punning to pathos, from melancholy to mad merriment,
sighing or laughing by the way at his readers or at himself
or at the stanzas. Into them he can fling anything under
the sun, from a doctor's prescription to a metaphysical
theory.

> When Bishop Berkeley said there was no matter,
> And proved it, 'twas no matter what he said,

is as cogent a refutation of idealism as the cumbrous wit
of Scotch logicians.

The popularity of the work is due not mainly to the
verbal skill which makes it rank as the *cleverest* of English
verse compositions, to its shoals of witticisms, its winged
words, telling phrases, and incomparable transitions ; but
to the fact that it continues to address a large class who

are not in the ordinary sense of the word lovers of poetry.
*Don Juan* is emphatically the poem of intelligent men of
middle age, who have grown weary of mere sentiment,
and yet retain enough of sympathetic feeling to desire
at times to recall it.  Such minds, crusted like Plato's
Glaucus with the world, are yet pervious to appeals to the
spirit that survives beneath the dry dust amid which
they move ; but only at rare intervals can they accompany the pure lyrist " singing as if he would never be
old," and they are apt to turn with some impatience even
from *Romeo and Juliet* to *Hamlet* and *Macbeth.*  To them,
on the other hand, the hard wit of *Hudibras* is equally
tiresome, and more distasteful ; their chosen friend is the
humourist who, inspired by a subtle perception of the con-
tradictions of life, sees matter for smiles in sorrow, and tears
in laughter.  Byron was not, in the highest sense, a great
humourist ; he does not blend together the two phases,
as they are blended in single sentences or whole chapters
of Sterne, in the April-sunshine of Richter, or in *Sartor
Resartus* ; but he comes near to produce the same effect
by his unequalled power of alternating them.  His
wit is seldom hard, never dry, for it is moistened by the
constant juxtaposition of sentiment.  His tenderness is
none the less genuine that he is perpetually jerking it
away—an equally favourite fashion with Carlyle,—as if he
could not trust himself to be serious for fear of becoming
sentimental ; and, in recollection of his frequent exhibitions
of unaffected hysteria, we accept his own confession—

> If I laugh at any mortal thing,
> 'Tis that I may not weep,

as a perfectly sincere comment on the most sincere, and
therefore in many respects the most effective, of his works.
He has, after his way, endeavoured in grave prose and

light verse to defend it against its assailants ; saying, "In
*Don Juan* I take a vicious and unprincipled character, and
lead him through those ranks of society whose accomplish-
ments cover and cloak their vices, and paint the natural
effects ;" and elsewhere, that he means to make his scamp
" end as a member of the Society for the Suppression of
Vice, or by the guillotine, or in an unhappy marriage." It
were easy to dilate on the fact that in interpreting the
phrases of the satirist into the language of the moralist we
often require to read them backwards : Byron's own statement, " I hate a motive," is, however, more to the point :

> But the fact is that I have nothing plann'd,
> Unless it were to be a moment merry—
> A novel word in my vocabulary.

*Don Juan* can only be credited with a text in the sense in
which every large experience, of its own accord, con-
veys its lesson. It was to the author a picture of the
world as he saw it ; and it is to us a mirror in which
every attribute of his genius, every peculiarity of his
nature, is reflected without distortion. After the auda-
cious though brilliant opening, and the unfortunately
pungent reference to the poet's domestic affairs, we find in
the famous storm (c. ii.) a bewildering epitome of his
prevailing manner. Home-sickness, sea-sickness, the
terror of the tempest, " wailing, blasphemy, devotion," the
crash of the wreck, the wild farewell, " the bubbling cry
of some strong swimmer in his agony," the horrors of
famine, the tale of the two fathers, the beautiful apparitions
of the rainbow and the bird, the feast on Juan's spaniel,
his reluctance to dine on " his pastor and his master,"
the consequences of eating Pedrillo,—all follow each
other like visions in the phantasmagoria of a nightmare,

till at last the remnant of the crew are drowned by a
ridiculous rhyme—

> Finding no place for their landing better,
> They ran the boat ashore,—and overset her.

Then comes the episode of Haidee, "a long low island
song of ancient days," the character of the girl herself
being like a thread of pure gold running through the fabric
of its surroundings, motley in every page; e.g., after the
impassioned close of the "Isles of Greece," we have the
stanza :—

> Thus sang, or would, or could, or should, have sung,
> The modern Greek, in tolerable verse;
> If not like Orpheus quite, when Greece was young,
> Yet in those days he might have done much worse—

with which the author dashes away the romance of the
song, and then launches into a tirade against Bob
Southey's epic and Wordsworth's pedlar poems. This
vein exhausted, we come to the "Ave Maria," one of the
most musical, and seemingly heartfelt, hymns in the
language. The close of the ocean pastoral (in c. iv.) is the
last of pathetic narrative in the book; but the same feeling
that "mourns o'er the beauty of the Cyclades," often re-
emerges in shorter passages. The fifth and sixth cantos,
in spite of the glittering sketch of Gulbeyaz, and the fawn-
like image of Dudù, are open to the charge of diffuseness,
and the character of Johnson is a failure. From the
seventh to the tenth, the poem decidedly dips, partly
because the writer had never been in Russia; then it
again rises, and shows no sign of falling off to the end.

No part of the work has more suggestive interest or
varied power than some of the later cantos, in which Juan
is whirled through the vortex of the fashionable life which

N

Byron knew so well, loved so much, and at last esteemed
so little. There is no richer piece of descriptive writing
in his works than that of Newstead (in c. xiii.) ; nor is
there any analysis of female character so subtle as that
of the Lady Adeline. Conjectures as to the originals of
imaginary portraits, are generally futile ; but Miss Mill-
pond—not Donna Inez—is obviously Lady Byron ; in
Adeline we may suspect that at Genoa he was drawing
from the life in the Villa Paradiso ; while Aurora Raby
seems to be an idealization of La Guiccioli :—

> Early in years, and yet more infantine
>   In figure, she had something of sublime
> In eyes, which sadly shone, as seraphs' shine :
>   All youth—but with an aspect beyond time ;
> Radiant and grave—as pitying man's decline ;
>   Mournful—but mournful of another's crime,
> She look'd as if she sat by Eden's door,
> And grieved for those who could return no more.
>
> She was a Catholic, too, sincere, austere,
>   As far as her own gentle heart allow'd,
> And deem'd that fallen worship far more dear,
>   Perhaps, because 'twas fallen : her sires were proud
> Of deeds and days, when they had fill'd the ear
>   Of nations, and had never bent or bow'd
> To novel power ; and, as she was the last,
> She held her old faith and old feelings fast.
>
> She gazed upon a world she scarcely knew,
>   As seeking not to know it ; silent, lone,
> As grows a flower, thus quietly she grew,
>   And kept her heart serene within its zone.

Constantly, towards the close of the work, there is an
echo of home and country, a half involuntary cry after—

> The love of higher things and better days ;
>   Th' unbounded hope, and heavenly ignorance
> Of what is call'd the world and the world's ways.

In the concluding stanza of the last completed canto,
beginning—

> Between two worlds life hovers like a star,
> 'Twixt night and morn, on the horizon's verge—

we have a condensation of the refrain of the poet's philosophy; but the main drift of the later books is a satire on
London society.  There are elements in a great city which
may be wrought into something nobler than satire, for all
the energies of the age are concentrated where passion is
fiercest and thought intensest, amid the myriad sights and
sounds of its glare and gloom.  But those scenes, and the
actors in them, are apt also to induce the frame of mind in
which a prose satirist describes himself as reclining under
an arcade of the Pantheon : "Not the Pantheon by the
Piazza Navona, where the immortal gods were worshipped
—the immortal gods now dead; but the Pantheon in
Oxford Street. Have not Selwyn, and Walpole, and March,
and Carlisle figured there ?  Has not Prince Florizel
flounced through the hall in his rustling domino, and
danced there in powdered splendour ?  O my companions,
I have drunk many a bout with you, and always found
'Vanitas Vanitatum' written on the bottom of the pot."
This is the mind in which *Don Juan* interprets the universe, and paints the still living court of Florizel and his
buffoons.  A "nondescript and ever varying rhyme"—
"a versified aurora borealis," half cynical, half Epicurean,
it takes a partial though a subtle view of that microcosm
on stilts called the great world.  It complains that in the
days of old "men made the manners—manners now make
men."  It concludes—

> Good company's a chess-board, there are kings,
> Queens, bishops, knights, rooks, pawns; the world's a game.

It passes from a reflection on " the dreary *fuimus* of all things here " to the advice—

> But "carpo diem," Juan, "carpe, carpe! "
> To-morrow sees another race as gay
> And transient, and devour'd by the same harpy.
> " Life's a poor player,"—then play out the play.

It was the natural conclusion of the foregone stage of Byron's career. Years had given him power, but they were years in which his energies were largely wasted. Self-indulgence had not petrified his feeling, but it had thrown wormwood into its springs. He had learnt to look on existence as a walking shadow, and was strong only with the strength of a sincere despair.

> Through life's road, so dim and dirty,
> I have dragg'd to three and thirty.
> What have those years left to me ?
> Nothing, except thirty-three.

These lines are the summary of one who had drained the draught of pleasure to the dregs of bitterness.

# CHAPTER X.

## 1821—1824.

In leaving Venice for Ravenna, Byron passed from the
society of gondoliers and successive sultanas to a comparatively domestic life, with a mistress who at least
endeavoured to stimulate some of his higher aspirations,
and smiled upon his wearing the sword along with the
lyre.  In the last episode of his constantly chequered and
too voluptuous career, we have the waking of Sardanapalus
realized in the transmutation of the fantastical Harold
into a practical strategist, financier, and soldier.  No one
ever lived who, in the same space, more thoroughly ran
the gauntlet of existence.  Having exhausted all other
sources of vitality and intoxication—travel, gallantry, and
verse—it remained for the despairing poet to become a
hero.  But he was also moved by a public passion, the
genuineness of which there is no reasonable ground to
doubt.  Like Alfieri and Rousseau, he had taken for his
motto, " I am of the opposition ; " and, as Dante under a
republic called for a monarchy, Byron, under monarchies
at home and abroad, called for a commonwealth.  Amid
the inconsistencies of his political sentiment, he had been
consistent in so much love of liberty as led him to
denounce oppression, even when he had no great faith

in the oppressed—whether English, or Italians, or Greeks.

Byron regarded the established dynasties of the continent with a sincere hatred. He talks of the "more than infernal tyranny" of the House of Austria. To his fancy, as to Shelley's, New England is the star of the future. Attracted by a strength or rather force of character akin to his own, he worshipped Napoleon, even when driven to confess that "the hero had sunk into a king." He lamented his overthrow ; but, above all, that he was beaten by "three stupid, legitimate old dynasty boobies of regular sovereigns." "I write in ipecacuanha that the Bourbons are restored." "What right have we to prescribe laws to France? Here we are retrograding to the dull, stupid old system, balance of Europe—poising straws on kings' noses, instead of wringing them off." "The king-times are fast finishing. There will be blood shed like water, and tears like mist ; but the peoples will conquer in the end. I shall not live to see it, but I foresee it." "Give me a republic. Look in the history of the earth—Rome, Greece, Venice, Holland, France, America, our too short Commonwealth—and compare it with what they did under masters."

His serious political verses are all in the strain of the lines on Wellington—

> Never had mortal man such opportunity—
> Except Napoleon—or abused it more ;
> You might have freed fallen Europe from the unity
> Of tyrants, and been blessed from shore to shore.

An enthusiasm for Italy, which survived many disappointments, dictated some of the most impressive passages of his *Harold*, and inspired the *Lament of Tasso* and the

*Ode on Venice.* The *Prophecy of Dante* contains much
that has since proved prophetic—

> What is there wanting, then, to set thee free,
> And show thy beauty in its fullest light ?
> To make the Alps impassable ; and we,
> Her sons, may do this with one deed—*Unite !*

His letters reiterate the same idea, in language even
more emphatic. "It is no great matter, supposing that
Italy could be liberated, who or what is sacrificed. It is
a grand object—the very poetry of politics : only think—
a free Italy ! " Byron acted on his assertion that a man
ought to do more for society than write verses. Mistrusting
its leaders, and detesting the wretched lazzaroni, who
" would have betrayed themselves and all the world," he
yet threw himself heart and soul into the insurrection of
1820, saying, " Whatever I can do by money, means, or
person, I will venture freely for their freedom." He
joined the secret society of the Carbonari, wrote an address
to the Liberal government set up in Naples, supplied arms
and a refuge in his house, which he was prepared to con-
vert into a fortress. In February, 1821, on the rout of the
Neapolitans by the Austrians, the conspiracy was crushed.
Byron, who " had always an idea that it would be
bungled," expressed his fear that the country would be
thrown back for 500 years into barbarism, and the
Countess Guiccioli confessed with tears that the Italians
must return to composing and strumming operatic airs.
Carbonarism having collapsed, it of course made way for a
reaction ; but the encouragement and countenance of the
English poet and peer helped to keep alive the smouldering fire that Mazzini fanned into a flame, till Cavour
turned it to a practical purpose, and the dreams of the
idealists of 1820 were finally realized.

On the failure of the luckless conspiracy, Byron naturally betook himself to history, speculation, satire, and
ideas of a journalistic propaganda ; but all through, his
mind was turning to the renewal of the action which was
his destiny. "If I live ten years longer," he writes
in 1822, "you will see that it is not all over with me.
I don't mean in literature, for that is nothing—and I do
not think it was my vocation ; but I shall do something."
The Greek war of liberation opened a new field for the
exercise of his indomitable energy. This romantic struggle,
begun in April, 1821, was carried on for two years with
such remarkable success, that at the close of 1822 Greece
was beginning to be recognized as an independent state :
but in the following months the tide seemed to turn ;
dissensions broke out among the leaders, the spirit of
intrigue seemed to stifle patriotism, and the energies of the
insurgents were hampered for want of the sinews of war.
There was a danger of the movement being starved out, and
the committee of London sympathizers—of which the poet's
intimate friend and frequent correspondent, Mr. Douglas
Kinnaird, and Captain Blaquière, were leading promoters
—was impressed with the necessity of procuring funds in
support of the cause. With a view to this it seemed of
consequence to attach to it some shining name, and men's
thoughts almost inevitably turned to Byron. No other
Englishman seemed so fit to be associated with the enterprise as the warlike poet, who had twelve years before
linked his fame to that of "grey Marathon" and "Athena's
tower," and, more recently immortalized the isles on which
he cast so many a longing glance. Hobhouse broke the
subject to him early in the spring of 1823: the committee opened communications in April. After hesi-
tating through May, in June Byron consented to meet

Blaquière at Zante, and, on hearing the results of the
captain's expedition to the Morea, to decide on future
steps. His share in this enterprise has been assigned
to purely personal and comparatively mean motives. He
was, it is said, disgusted with his periodical, sick of his
editor, tired of his mistress, and bent on any change, from
China to Peru, that would give him a new theatre for
display. One grows weary of the perpetual half-truths of
inveterate detraction. It is granted that Byron was rest-
less, vain, imperious, never did anything without a desire
to shine in the doing of it, and was to a great degree the
slave of circumstances. Had the *Liberal* proved a lamp
to the nations, instead of a mere " red flag flaunted in the
face of John Bull," he might have cast anchor at Genoa;
but the whole drift of his work and life demonstrates
that he was capable on occasion of merging himself in
what he conceived to be great causes, especially in their
evil days. Of the Hunts he may have had enough;
but the invidious statement about La Guiccioli has no
foundation, other than a somewhat random remark of
Shelley, and the fact that he left her nothing in his will.
It is distinctly ascertained that she expressly prohibited
him from doing so ; they continued to correspond to the
last, and her affectionate, though unreadable, reminiscences,
are sufficient proof that she at no time considered herself
to be neglected, injured, or aggrieved.

Byron indeed left Italy in an unsettled state of mind :
he spoke of returning in a few months, and as the period
for his departure approached, became more and more irre-
solute. A presentiment of his death seemed to brood
over a mind always superstitious, though never fanatical.
Shortly before his own departure, the Blessingtons
were preparing to leave Genoa for England. On the

evening of his farewell call he began to speak of his
voyage with despondency, saying, "Here we are all now
together ; but when and where shall we meet again ?  I
have a sort of boding that we see each other for the last
time, as something tells me I shall never again return
from Greece :" after which remark he leant his head on
the sofa, and burst into one of his hysterical fits of tears.
The next week was given to preparations for an expedition,
which, entered on with mingled motives—sentimental,
personal, public—became more real and earnest to Byron
at every step he took.  He knew all the vices of the
" hereditary bondsmen" among whom he was going, and
went among them, with yet unquenched aspirations,
but with the bridle of discipline in his hand, resolved
to pave the way towards the nation becoming better, by
devoting himself to making it free.

On the morning of July 14th (1823) he embarked in
the brig "Hercules," with Trelawny, Count Pietro Gamba,
who remained with him to the last, Bruno a young
Italian doctor, Scott the captain of the vessel, and
eight servants, including Fletcher, besides the crew.
They had on board two guns, with other arms and ammu-
nition, five horses, an ample supply of medicines, with
50,000 Spanish dollars in coin and bills.  The start was
inauspicious.  A violent squall drove them back to port,
and in the course of a last ride with Gamba to Albaro,
Byron asked, "Where shall we be in a year?"  On the
same day of the same month of 1824 he was carried to
the tomb of his ancestors.  They again set sail on the
following evening, and in five days reached Leghorn,
where the poet received a salutation in verse, addressed
to him by Goethe, and replied to it.  Here Mr. Hamilton
Brown, a Scotch gentleman with considerable knowledge of

Greek affairs, joined the party, and induced them to change
their course to Cephalonia, for the purpose of obtaining
the advice and assistance of the English resident, Colonel
Napier. The poet occupied himself during the voyage
mainly in reading—among other books, Scott's *Life of
Swift*, Grimm's *Correspondence*, La Rochefoucauld, and
Las Casas—and watching the classic or historic shores
which they skirted, especially noting Elba, Soracte, the
Straits of Messina, and Etna. In passing Stromboli he
said to Trelawny, "You will see this scene in a fifth
canto of *Childe Harold*." On his companions suggesting
that he should write some verses on the spot, he tried to
do so, but threw them away, with the remark, "I cannot
write poetry at will, as you smoke tobacco." Trelawny
confesses that he was never on shipboard with a better
companion, and that a severer test of good fellowship it is
impossible to apply. Together they shot at gulls or empty
bottles, and swam every morning in the sea. Early in
August they reached their destination. Coming in sight
of the Morea, the poet said to Trelawny, "I feel as if
the eleven long years of bitterness I have passed through,
since I was here, were taken from my shoulders, and I
was scudding through the Greek Archipelago with old
Bathurst in his frigate." Byron remained at or about
Cephalonia till the close of the year. Not long after his
arrival he made an excursion to Ithaca, and, visiting the
monastery at Vathi, was received by the abbot with
great ceremony, which, in a fit of irritation, brought on by
a tiresome ride on a mule, he returned with unusual dis-
courtesy; but next morning, on his giving a donation to
their alms-box, he was dismissed with the blessing of the
monks. "If this isle were mine," he declared on his way
back, "I would break my staff and bury my book." A

little later, Brown and Trelawny being sent off with
letters to the provisional government, the former returned
with some Greek emissaries to London, to negotiate a
loan ; the latter attached himself to Odysseus, the chief
of the republican party at Athens, and never again saw
Byron alive.  The poet, after spending a month on board
the " Hercules," dismissed the vessel, and hired a house
for Gamba and himself at Metaxata, a healthy village
about four miles from the capital of the island.  Meanwhile, Blaquière, neglecting his appointment at Zante,
had gone to Corfu, and thence to England.  Colonel
Napier being absent from Cephalonia, Byron had some
pleasant social intercourse with his deputy, but, unable
to get from him any authoritative information, was left
without advice, to be besieged by letters and messages
from the factions.  Among these there were brought to
him hints that the Greeks wanted a king, and he is
reported to have said, " If they make me the offer, I will
perhaps not reject it."

The position would doubtless have been acceptable to a
man who never—amid his many self-deceptions—affected
to deny that he was ambitious : and who can say what
might not have resulted for Greece, had the poet lived to
add lustre to her crown ?  In the meantime, while faring
more frugally than a day-labourer, he yet surrounded
himself with a show of royal state, had his servants armed
with gilt helmets, and gathered around him a body-guard
of Suliotes.  These wild mercenaries becoming turbulent,
he was obliged to despatch them to Mesolonghi, then
threatened with siege by the Turks and anxiously waiting
relief.  During his residence at Cephalonia, Byron was
gratified by the interest evinced in him by the English
residents.  Among these the physician, Dr. Kennedy, a

worthy Scotchman, who imagined himself to be a theologian with a genius for conversion, was conducting a
series of religious meetings at Argostoli, when the poet
expressed a wish to be present at one of them.  After
listening, it is said, to a set of discourses that occupied
the greater part of twelve hours, he seems, for one reason or another, to have felt called on to enter the
lists, and found himself involved in the series of controversial dialogues afterwards published in a substantial book.   This volume, interesting in several respects, is
one of the most charming examples of unconscious irony
in the language, and it is matter of regret that our space
does not admit of the abridgment of several of its pages.
They bear testimony, on the one hand, to Byron's capability
of patience, and frequent sweetness of temper under trial ;
on the other, to Kennedy's utter want of humour, and
to his courageous honesty.   The curiously confronted
interlocutors, in the course of the missionary and
subsequent private meetings, ran over most of the
ground debated between opponents and apologists of
the Calvinistic faith, which Kennedy upheld without
stint.   The *Conversations* add little to what we already
know of Byron's religious opinions; nor is it easy to
say where he ceases to be serious and begins to banter,
or vice versâ.   He evidently wished to show that in
argument he was good at fence, and could handle a
theologian as skilfully as a foil.   At the same time he
wished if possible, though, as appears, in vain, to get
some light on a subject with regard to which in his graver
moods he was often exercised.   On some points he is
explicit.   He makes an unequivocal protest against the
doctrines of eternal punishment and infant damnation,
saying that if the rest of mankind were to be damned,

he "would rather keep them company than creep into
heaven alone." On questions of inspiration, and the
deeper problems of human life, he is less distinct,
being naturally inclined to a speculative necessita-
rianism, and disposed to admit original depravity;
but he did not see his way out of the maze through the
Atonement, and held that prayer had only significance
as a devotional affection of the heart. Byron showed a
remarkable familiarity with the Scriptures, and with parts
of Barrow, Chillingworth, and Stillingfleet; but on Kennedy's lending for his edification Boston's *Fourfold State*, he
returned it with the remark that it was too deep for him.
On another occasion he said, " Do you know I am nearly
reconciled to St. Paul, for he says there is no difference between the Jews and the Greeks? and I am exactly of the
same opinion, for the character of both is equally vile."
The good Scotchman's religious self-confidence is throughout free from intellectual pride; and his own confession,
"This time I suspect his lordship had the best of it,"
might perhaps be applied to the whole discussion.

Critics who have little history and less war have been
accustomed to attribute Byron's lingering at Cephalonia to
indolence and indecision; they write as if he ought on
landing on Greek soil to have put himself at the head of
an army and stormed Constantinople. Those who know
more, confess that the delay was deliberate, and that it was
judicious. The Hellenic uprising was animated by the
spirit of a " lion after slumber," but it had the heads of a
Hydra hissing and tearing at one another. The chiefs who
defended the country by their arms, compromised her by
their arguments, and some of her best fighters were little
better than pirates and bandits. Greece was a prey to
factions—republican, monarchic, aristocratic—representing

naval, military, and territorial interests, and each beset by
the adventurers who flock round every movement, only representing their own. During the first two years of success
they were held in embryo ; during the later years of disaster,
terminated by the allies at Navarino, they were buried ;
during the interlude of Byron's residence, when the foes
were like hounds in the leash, waiting for a renewal of the
struggle, they were rampant. Had he joined any one of
them he would have degraded himself to the level of a
mere condottiere, and helped to betray the common cause.
Beset by solicitations to go to Athens, to the Morea, to
Acarnania, he resolutely held apart, biding his time, collecting information, making himself known as a man of
affairs, endeavouring to conciliate rival clamants for
pension or place, and carefully watching the tide of
war. Numerous anecdotes of the period relate to
acts of public or private benevolence, which endeared
him to the population of the island; but he was on
the alert against being fleeced or robbed. " The
bulk of the English," writes Colonel Napier, " came ex-
pecting to find the Peloponnesus filled with Plutarch's
men, and returned thinking the inhabitants of Newgate
more moral. Lord Byron judged the Greeks fairly, and
knew that allowance must be made for emancipated slaves."
Among other incidents we hear of his passing a group, who
were "shrieking and howling as in Ireland" over some men
buried in the fall of a bank ; he snatched a spade, began
to dig, and threatened to horsewhip the peasants unless
they followed his example. On November 30th he
despatched to the central government a remarkable state
paper, in which he dwells on the fatal calamity of a civil
war, and says that unless union and order are established
all hopes of a loan—which being every day more urgent,

he was in letters to England constantly pressing—are at
an end. " I desire," he concluded, " the wellbeing of
Greece, and nothing else. I will do all I can to secure
it ; but I will never consent that the English public
be deceived as to the real state of affairs. You have
fought gloriously ; act honourably towards your fellow-
citizens and the world, and it will then no more be said,
as has been repeated for two thousand years, with the
Roman historians, that Philopœmen was the last of the
Grecians."

Prince Alexander Mavrocordatos—the most prominent
of the practical patriotic leaders—having been deposed
from the presidency, was sent to regulate the affairs
of Western Greece, and was now on his way with a
fleet to relieve Mesolonghi, in attempting which the
brave Marco Bozzaris had previously fallen. In a
letter, opening communication with a man for whom
he always entertained a high esteem, Byron writes,
" Colonel Stanhope has arrived from London, charged
by our committee to act in concert with me. . . . . .
Greece is at present placed between three measures—
either to reconquer her liberty, to become a depen-
dence of the sovereigns of Europe, or to return to
a Turkish province. She has the choice only of these
three alternatives. Civil war is but a road that leads to
the two latter."

At length the long looked-for fleet arrived, and the
Turkish squadron, with the loss of a treasure-ship,
retired up the Gulf of Lepanto. Mavrocordatos on
entering Mesolonghi lost no time in inviting the poet
to join him, and placed a brig at his disposal, adding,
" I need not tell you to what a pitch your presence is
desired by everybody, or what a prosperous direction

it will give to all our affairs. Your counsels will be
listened to like oracles."

At the same date Stanhope writes, "The people in
the streets are looking forward to his lordship's arrival
as they would to the coming of the Messiah." Byron
was unable to start in the ship sent for him; but
in spite of medical warnings, a few days later, i. e.
December 28th, he embarked in a small fast-sailing
sloop called a mistico, while the servants and baggage were stowed in another and larger vessel under
the charge of Count Gamba. From Gamba's graphic account of the voyage we may take the following :—" We
sailed together till after ten at night; the wind favourable, a clear sky, the air fresh, but not sharp. Our
sailors sang alternately patriotic songs, monotonous indeed, but to persons in our situation extremely touching, and we took part in them. We were all, but Lord
Byron particularly, in excellent spirits. The mistico
sailed the fastest. When the waves divided us, and our
voices could no longer reach each other, we made signals
by firing pistols and carbines. To-morrow we meet at
Mesolonghi—to morrow. Thus, full of confidence and
spirits, we sailed along. At twelve we were out of sight
of each other."

Byron's vessel, separated from her consort, came into
the close proximity of a Turkish frigate, and had to
take refuge among the Scrofes' rocks. Emerging thence,
he attained a small seaport of Acarnania, called Dra-
gomestri, whence sallying forth on the 2nd of January
under the convoy of some Greek gunboats, he was
nearly wrecked. On the 4th Byron made, when violently heated, an imprudent plunge in the sea, and was
never afterwards free from a pain in his bones. On the

o

5th he arrived at Mesolonghi, and was received with salvoes
of musketry and music. Gamba was waiting him. His
vessel, the "Bombarda," had been taken by the
Ottoman frigate, but the captain of the latter, recognizing the Count as having formerly saved his life in
the Black Sea, made interest in his behalf with Yussuf
Pasha at Patras, and obtained his discharge. In recom-
pense, the poet subsequently sent to the Pasha some
Turkish prisoners, with a letter requesting him to en-
deavour to mitigate the inhumanities of the war. Byron
brought to the Greeks at Mesolonghi the 4000*l.* of his
personal loan (applied, in the first place, to defraying the
expenses of the fleet), with the spell of his name and
presence. He was shortly afterwards appointed to the
command of the intended expedition against Lepanto,
and, with this view, again took into his pay five
hundred Suliotes. An approaching general assembly to
organize the forces of the west, had brought together a
motley crew, destitute, discontented, and more likely to
wage war upon each other than on their enemies. Byron's
closest associates during the ensuing months, were the
engineer Parry, an energetic artilleryman, "extremely
active, and of strong practical talents," who had travelled
in America, and Colonel Stanhope (afterwards Lord
Harrington) equally with himself devoted to the emancipation of Greece, but at variance about the means of
achieving it. Stanhope, a moral enthusiast of the stamp
of Kennedy, beset by the fallacy of religious missions,
wished to cover the Morea with Wesleyan tracts, and
liberate the country by the agency of the Press. He had
imported a converted blacksmith, with a cargo of Bibles,
types, and paper, who on 20*l.* a year, undertook to
accomplish the reform. Byron, backed by the good sense

of Mavrocordatos, proposed to make cartridges of the
tracts, and small shot of the type; he did not think that
the turbulent tribes were ripe for freedom of the press,
and had begun to regard Republicanism itself as a matter
of secondary moment.   The disputant allies in the
common cause occupied each a flat of the same small house,
the soldier by profession was bent on writing the Turks
down, the poet on fighting them down, holding that " the
work of the sword must precede that of the pen, and that
camps must  be the training schools of freedom."   Their
altercations were sometimes fierce—" Despot !" cried Stanhope, "after professing liberal principles from boyhood, you
when called to act prove yourself a Turk."  " Radical !" re-
torted Byron, " if I had held up my finger I could have
crushed your press,"—but this did not prevent the recognition by each of them of the excellent qualities of the other.

Ultimately Stanhope went to Athens, and allied himself
with Trelawny and Odysseus and the party of the Left.
Nothing can be more statesmanlike than some of Byron's
papers of this and the immediately preceding period; nothing more admirable than the spirit which inspires them.
He had come into the heart of a revolution, exposed to the
same perils as those which had wrecked the similar movement in Italy.   Neither trusting too much nor distrusting
too much, with a clear head and a good will he set about
enforcing a series of excellent measures.   From first to
last he was engaged in denouncing dissension, in advo-
cating unity, in doing everything that man could do to
concentrate and utilize the disorderly elements with which
he had to work.   He occupied himself in repairing forti-
fications, managing ships, restraining licence, promoting
courtesy between the foes, and regulating the disposal of
the sinews of war.

On the morning of the 22nd of January, his last birthday,
he came from his room to Stanhope's, and said, smiling,
" You were complaining that I never write any poetry
now," and read the familiar stanzas beginning—

> 'Tis time this heart should be unmoved,

and ending—

> Seek out – less often sought than found—
> A soldier's grave, for thee the best;
> Then look around, and choose thy ground,
> And take thy rest.

High thoughts, high resolves ; but the brain that was over-
tasked, and the frame that was outworn, would be tasked
and worn little longer. The lamp of a life that had burnt
too fiercely was flickering to its close. " If we are not
taken off with the sword," he writes on February 5th, " we
are like to march off with an ague in this mud basket ;
and, to conclude with a very bad pun, better *martially*
than *marsh-ally*. The dykes of Holland when broken
down are the deserts of Arabia, in comparison with Mesolonghi." In April, when it was too late, Stanhope wrote
from Salona, in Phocis, imploring him not to sacrifice
health, and perhaps life, " in that bog."

Byron's house stood in the midst of the exhalations of
a muddy creek, and his natural irritability was increased
by a more than usually long ascetic regimen. From the
day of his arrival in Greece he discarded animal food and
lived mainly on toast, vegetables, and cheese, olives and
light wine, at the rate of forty paras a day. In spite of
his strength of purpose, his temper was not always proof
against the rapacity and turbulence by which he was surrounded. About the middle of February, when the artil-
lery had been got into readiness for the attack on Lepanto

—the northern, as Patras was the southern, gate of the
gulf, still in the hands of the Turks—the expedition was
thrown back by an unexpected rising of the Suliotes.
These peculiarly froward Greeks, chronically seditious by
nature, were on this occasion, as afterwards appeared,
stirred up by emissaries of Colocatroni, who, though
assuming the position of the rival of Mavrocordatos, was
simply a brigand on a large scale in the Morea. Exas-
peration at this mutiny, and the vexation of having to
abandon a cherished scheme, seem to have been the immediately provoking causes of a violent convulsive fit which,
on the evening of the 15th, attacked the poet, and endan-
gered his life. Next day he was better, but complained
of weight in the head ; and the doctors applying leeches
too close to the temporal artery, he was bled till he fainted.
And now occurred the last of those striking incidents so
frequent in his life, in reference to which we may quote
the joint testimony of two witnesses. Colonel Stanhope
writes, " Soon after his dreadful paroxysm, when he was
lying on his sick-bed, with his whole nervous system completely shaken, the mutinous Suliotes, covered with dirt
and splendid attires, broke into his apartment, brandish-
ing their costly arms and loudly demanding their rights.
Lord Byron, electrified by this unexpected act, seemed to
recover from his sickness ; and the more the Suliotes
raged, the more his calm courage triumphed. The scene
was truly sublime." " It is impossible," says Count
Gamba, " to do justice to the coolness and magnanimity
which he displayed upon every trying occasion. Upon
trifling occasions he was certainly irritable ; but the aspect
of danger calmed him in an instant, and restored him the
free exercise of all the powers of his noble nature. A
more undaunted man in the hour of peril never breathed."

A few days later, the riot being renewed, the disorderly
crew were, on payment of their arrears, finally dismissed;
but several of the English artificers under Parry left
about the same time, in fear of their lives.

On the 4th, the last of the long list of Byron's letters
to Moore resents, with some bitterness, the hasty
acceptance of a rumour that he had been quietly writing
*Don Juan* in some Ionian island. At the same date
he writes to Kennedy, "I am not unaware of the pre-
carious state of my health. But it is proper I should
remain in Greece, and it were better to die doing
something than nothing." Visions of enlisting Europe
and America on behalf of the establishment of a new
state, that might in course of time develope itself over
the realm of Alexander, floated and gleamed in his fancy;
but in his practical daily procedure the poet took as
his text the motto "festina lente," insisted on solid
ground under his feet, and had no notion of sailing
balloons over the sea. With this view he discouraged
Stanhope's philanthropic and propagandist paper, the
*Telegrapho*, and disparaged Dr. Mayer, its Swiss editor,
saying, "Of all petty tyrants he is one of the pettiest,
as are most demagogues." Byron had none of the
Sclavonic leanings, and almost personal hatred of
Ottoman rule, of some of our statesmen; but he saw on
what side lay the forces and the hopes of the future.
"I cannot calculate," he said to Gamba, during one of
their latest rides together, "to what a height Greece
may rise. Hitherto it has been a subject for the hymns
and elegies of fanatics and enthusiasts; but now it will
draw the attention of the politician. . . . At present
there is little difference, in many respects, between
Greeks and Turks, nor could there be; but the latter

must, in the common course of events, decline in power ;
and the former must as inevitably become better. . . .
The English Government deceived itself at first in
thinking it possible to maintain the Turkish Empire in
its integrity ; but it cannot be done, that unwieldy mass
is already putrified, and must dissolve.   If anything
like an equilibrium is to be upheld, Greece must be sup-
ported." These words have been well characterized as
prophetic.  During this time Byron rallied in health,
and displayed much of his old spirit, vivacity, and
humour, took part in such of his favourite amusements
as circumstances admitted, fencing, shooting, riding, and
playing with his pet dog Lion.   The last of his recorded
practical jokes is his rolling about cannon balls, and
shaking the rafters, to frighten Parry in the room below
with the dread of an earthquake.

Towards the close of the month, after being solicited to
accompany Mavrocordatos, to share the governorship of the
Morea, he made an appointment to meet Colonel Stanhope
and Odysseus at Salona, but was prevented from keeping
it by violent floods which blocked up the communication.
On the 30th he was presented with the freedom of the
city of Mesolonghi.   On the 3rd of April he intervened
to prevent an Italian private, guilty of theft, from being
flogged by order of some German officers.   On the 9th, ex-
hilarated by a letter from Mrs. Leigh with good accounts
of her own and Ada's health, he took a long ride with
Gamba and a few of the remaining Suliotes, and after being
violently heated, and then drenched in a heavy shower,
persisted in returning home in a boat, remarking with
a laugh, in answer to a remonstrance, " I should make
a pretty soldier if I were to care for such a trifle."
It soon became apparent that he had caught his death.

Almost immediately on his return, he was seized with
shiverings and violent pain. The next day he rose as
usual, and had his last ride in the olive woods. On
the 11th a rheumatic fever set in. On the 14th,
Bruno's skill being exhausted, it was proposed to call
Dr. Thomas from Zante, but a hurricane prevented
any ship being sent. On the 15th, another physician,
Mr. Milligen, suggested bleeding to allay the fever,
but Byron held out against it, quoting Dr. Reid to
the effect that "less slaughter is effected by the lance
than the lancet—that minute instrument of mighty mischief;" and saying to Bruno, "If my hour is come I shall
die, whether I lose my blood or keep it." Next morning
Milligen induced him to yield, by a suggestion of the
possible loss of his reason. Throwing out his arm, he cried,
"There! you are, I see, a d—d set of butchers. Take
away as much blood as you like, and have done with it."
The remedy, repeated on the following day with blistering,
was either too late or ill-advised. On the 18th he saw
more doctors, but was manifestly sinking, amid the tears
and lamentations of attendants who could not understand
each other's language. In his last hours his delirium
bore him to the field of arms. He fancied he was leading
the attack on Lepanto, and was heard exclaiming, "Forwards! forwards! follow me!" Who is not reminded of
another death-bed, not remote in time from his, and the
*Tête d'armée* of the great Emperor who with the great Poet
divided the wonder of Europe? The stormy vision passed,
and his thoughts reverted home. "Go to my sister,"
he faltered out to Fletcher; "tell her—go to Lady Byron
—you will see her, and say"—nothing more could be heard
but broken ejaculations: "Augusta—Ada—my sister, my
child. Io lascio qualche cosa di caro nel mondo. For the

rest, I am content to die." At six on the evening of the
18th he uttered his last words, " Δεῖ με νῦν καθεύδειν ;"
and on the 19th he passed away.

Never perhaps was there such a national lamentation.
By order of Mavrocordatos, thirty-seven guns—one for
each year of the poet's life—were fired from the battery, and
answered by the Turks from Patras with an exultant volley.
All offices, tribunals, and shops were shut, and a general
mourning for twenty-one days proclaimed.    Stanhope
wrote, on hearing the news, "England has lost her
brightest genius—Greece her noblest friend;" and
Trelawny, on coming to Mesolonghi, heard nothing in the
streets but "Byron is dead!" like a bell tolling through
the silence and the gloom.    Intending contributors to the
cause of Greece turned back when they heard the tidings,
that seemed to them to mean she was headless.    Her
cities contended for the body, as of old for the birth of a
poet.    Athens wished him to rest in the Temple of
Theseus.    The funeral service was performed at Mesolonghi.    But on the 2nd of May the embalmed remains
left Zante, and on the 29th arrived in the Downs.    His
relatives applied for permission to have them interred in
Westminster Abbey, but it was refused ; and on the 16th
July they were conveyed to the village church of Hucknall.

# CHAPTER XI.

## CHARACTERISTICS, AND PLACE IN LITERATURE.

LORD JEFFREY at the close of a once-famous review quaintly laments: "The tuneful quartos of Southey are already little better than lumber, and the rich melodies of Keats and Shelley, and the fantastical emphasis of Wordsworth, and the plebeian pathos of Crabbe, are melting fast from the field of our vision. The novels of Scott have put out his poetry, and the blazing star of Byron himself is receding from its place of pride." Of the poets of the early part of this century, Lord John Russell thought Byron the greatest, then Scott, then Moore. "Such an opinion," wrote a *National* reviewer, in 1860, "is not worth a refutation; we only smile at it." Nothing in the history of literature is more curious than the shifting of the standard of excellence, which so perplexes criticism. But the most remarkable feature of the matter is the frequent return to power of the once discarded potentates. Byron is resuming his place: his spirit has come again to our atmosphere; and every budding critic, as in 1820, feels called onto pronounce a verdict on his genius and character. The present times are, in many respects, an aftermath of the first quarter of the century, which was an era of revolt, of doubt, of storm. There succeeded an era of exhaustion, of quiescence, of reflection. The first years of the third quarter saw a revival of turbulence and agitation; and, more than our fathers, we are inclined to sympathize with our grandfathers. Macaulay has popularized the story of the change of literary dynasty which in our island marked the close of the last, and the first two decades of the present, hundred years.

The corresponding artistic revolt on the continent was closely connected with changes in the political world. The originators of the romantic literature in Italy, for the most part, died in Spielberg or in exile. The same revolution which levelled the Bastille, and converted Versailles and the Trianon—the classic school in stone and terrace—into a moral Herculaneum and Pompeii, drove the models of the so-called Augustan ages into a museum of antiquarians. In our own country, the movement initiated by Chatterton, Cowper, and Burns, was carried out by two classes of great writers. They agreed in opposing freedom to formality; in substituting for the old, new aims and methods; in preferring a grain of mother wit to a peck of clerisy. They broke with the old school, as Protestantism broke with the old Church; but, like the sects, they separated again. Wordsworth, Southey, and Coleridge, while refusing to acknowledge the literary precedents of the past, submitted themselves to a self-imposed law. The partialities of their maturity were towards things settled and regulated; their favourite virtues, endurance and humility; their conformity to established institutions was the basis of a new Conservatism. The others were the Radicals of the movement : they practically acknowledged no law but their own inspiration. Dissatisfied with the existing order, their sympathies were with strong will and passion and defiant independence. These found their master-types in Shelley and in Byron.

A reaction is always an extreme. Lollards, Puritans, Covenanters, were in some respects nauseous antidotes to ecclesiastical corruption. The ruins of the Scotch cathedrals and of the French nobility are warnings at once against the excess that provokes and the excess that avenges. The revolt against the *ancien régime* in letters made possible the Ode that is the high-tide mark of modern English inspiration, but it was parodied in page on page of maundering rusticity. Byron saw the danger, but was borne headlong by the rapids. Hence the anomalous contrast between his theories and his performance. Both Wordsworth and Byron were bitten by Rousseau; but the former is, at furthest, a Girondin. The latter, acting like Danton on the motto "L'audace, l'audace, toujours l'audace," sighs after *Henri Quatre et Gabrièlle.* There is more of the spirit of the French Revolution in *Don Juan* than in all the works of the author's contemporaries; but his criticism is that of Boileau, and when deliberate is generally absurd. He never recognized the meaning of the artistic movement of his age, and overvalued those of his works which the Unities helped to destroy. He hailed Gifford as his Magnus Apollo, and put Rogers next to Scott in his comical pyramid. "Chaucer," he writes, "I think obscene and contemptible." He could see no merit in Spenser, preferred Tasso to Milton, and called the old English dramatists "mad and turbid mountebanks." In the same spirit he writes: "In the time of Pope it was all Horace, now it is all Claudian." He saw—what fanatics had begun to deny—that Pope was a great writer, and the "angel of reasonableness," the strong common sense of both was a link between them; but the expressions he uses during his controversy with Bowles look

like jests, till we are convinced of his earnestness by his
anger. "Neither time, nor distance, nor grief, nor age can
ever diminish my veneration for him who is the great
moral poet of all times, of all climes, of all feelings, and of
all stages of existence. . . . Your whole generation are
not worth a canto of the *Dunciad*, or anything that is
his." All the while he was himself writing prose and
verse, in grasp if not in vigour as far beyond the stretch
of Pope, as Pope is in "worth and wit and sense" removed
above his mimics. The point of the paradox is not merely
that he deserted, but that he sometimes imitated his
model, and when he did so, failed. Macaulay's judgment,
that "personal taste led him to the eighteenth century,
thirst for praise to the nineteenth," is quite at fault. There
can be no doubt that Byron loved praise as much as he affected to despise it. His note, on reading the *Quarterly* on
his dramas, "I am the most unpopular man in England," is
like the cry of a child under chastisement ; but he had
little affinity, moral or artistic, with the spirit of our so-
called Augustans, and his determination to admire them
was itself rebellious. Again we are reminded of his
phrase, "I am of the opposition." His vanity and pride
were perpetually struggling for the mastery, and though
he thirsted for popularity he was bent on compelling it ;
so he warred with the literary impulse of which he was
the child.

Byron has no relation to the master-minds whose
works reflect a nation or an era, and who keep their own
secrets. His verse and prose is alike biographical, and
the inequalities of his style are those of his career. He lived
in a glass case, and could not hide himself by his habit of
burning blue lights. He was too great to do violence to
his nature, which was not great enough to be really con-

sistent. It was thus natural for him to pose as the
spokesman of two ages—as a critic and as an author ; and
of two orders of society—as a peer, and as a poet of revolt.
Sincere in both, he could never forget the one character in
the other. To the last, he was an aristocrat in sentiment,
a democrat in opinion. "Vulgarity," he writes with a
pithy half-truth, "is far worse than downright black
guardism ; for the latter comprehends wit, humour, and
strong sense at times, while the former is a sad abortive
attempt at all things, signifying nothing." He could
never reconcile himself to the English radicals ; and it
has been acutely remarked, that part of his final interest
in Greece lay in the fact that he found it a country of
classic memories, " where a man might be the champion
of liberty without soiling himself in the arena." He
owed much of his early influence to the fact of his
moving in the circles of rank and fashion ; but though
himself steeped in the prejudices of caste, he struck
at them at times with fatal force. Aristocracy is the
individual asserting a vital distinction between itself and
"the muck o' the world." Byron's heroes all rebel against
the associative tendency of the nineteenth century ; they
are self-worshippers at war with society ; but most of them
come to bad ends. He maligned himself in those carica-
tures, and has given more of himself in describing one
whom with special significance we call a brother poet.
"Allen," he writes in 1813, "has lent me a quantity of
Burns's unpublished letters. . . . What an antithetical
mind !—tenderness, roughness — delicacy, coarseness—
sentiment, sensuality—soaring and grovelling—dirt and
deity—all mixed up in that one compound of inspired
clay !" We have only to add to these antitheses, in
applying them with slight modification to the writer.

Byron had, on occasion, more self-control than Burns, who yielded to every thirst or gust, and could never have lived the life of the soldier at Mesolonghi ; but partly owing to meanness, partly to a sound instinct, his memory has been more severely dealt with. The fact of his being a nobleman helped to make him famous, but it also helped to make him hated. No doubt it half spoiled him in making him a show; and the circumstance has suggested the remark of a humourist, that it is as hard for a lord to be a perfect gentleman as for a camel to pass through the needle's eye. But it also exposed to the rancours of jealousy a man who had nearly everything but domestic happiness to excite that most corroding of literary passions ; and when he got out of gear he became the quarry of Spenser's " blatant beast." On the other hand, Burns was, beneath his disgust at Holy Fairs and Willies, sincerely reverential ; much of *Don Juan* would have seemed to him " an atheist's laugh," and—a more certain superiority—he was absolutely frank.

Byron, like Pope, was given to playing monkey-like tricks, mostly harmless, but offensive to their victims. His peace of mind was dependent on what people would say of him, to a degree unusual even in the irritable race ; and when they spoke ill he was, again like Pope, essentially vindictive. The *Bards and Reviewers* beats about, where the lines to Atticus transfix with Philoctetes' arrows ; but they are due to a like impulse. Byron affected to contemn the world ; but, say what he would, he cared too much for it. He had a genuine love of solitude as an alterative ; but he could not subsist without society, and, Shelley tells us, wherever he went, became the nucleus of it. He sprang up again when flung to the earth, but he never attained to the disdain he desired.

We find him at once munificent and careful about
money ; calmly asleep amid a crowd of trembling sailors,
yet never going to ride without a nervous caution ;
defying augury, yet seriously disturbed by a gipsy's prattle.
He could be the most genial of comrades, the most considerate of masters, and he secured the devotion of his
servants, as of his friends ; but he was too overbearing to
form many equal friendships, and apt to be ungenerous to
his real rivals.  His shifting attitude towards Lady Byron,
his wavering purposes, his impulsive acts, are a part of
the character we trace through all his life and work,
—a strange mixture of magnanimity and brutality, of
laughter and tears, consistent in nothing but his passion and his pride, yet redeeming all his defects by
his graces, and wearing a greatness that his errors can only
half obscure.

Alternately the idol and the horror of his contemporaries, Byron was, during his life, feared and respected
as " the grand Napoleon of the realms of rhyme."  His
works were the events of the literary world.  The chief
among them were translated into French, German, Italian,
Danish, Polish, Russian, Spanish.  On the publication
of Moore's *Life*, Lord Macaulay had no hesitation in
referring to Byron as "the most celebrated Englishman
of the nineteenth century."  Nor have we now ; but
in the interval between 1840—1870, it was the fashion
to talk of him as a sentimentalist, a romancer, a shallow
wit, a nine days' wonder, a poet for " green unknowing
youth."  It was a reaction, such as leads us to dises-
tablish the heroes of our crude imaginations till we
learn that to admire nothing is as sure a sign of im-
maturity as to admire everything.

The weariness, if not disgust, induced by a throng of

more than usually absurd imitators, enabled Mr. Carlyle, the poet's successor in literary influence, more effectively to lead the counter-revolt. "In my mind," writes this critic, in 1839, " Byron has been sinking at an accelerated rate for the last ten years, and has now reached a very low level. . . . . His fame has been very great, but I do not see how it is to endure ; neither does that make him great. No genuine productive thought was ever revealed by him to mankind. He taught me nothing that I had not again to forget." The refrain of Carlyle's advice during the most active years of his criticism was, " Close thy Byron, open thy Goethe." We do so, and find that the refrain of Goethe's advice in reference to Byron is—" nocturnâ versate manu, versate diurnâ." He urged Eckermann to study English that he might read him ; remarking, " A character of such eminence has never existed before, and probably will never come again. The beauty of *Cain* is such as we shall not see a second time in the world. . . . Byron issues from the sea-waves ever fresh. I did right to present him with that monument of love in *Helena*. I could not make use of any man as the representative of the modern poetic era except him, who is undoubtedly to be regarded as the greatest genius of our century." Again : " Tasso's epic has maintained its fame, but Byron is the burning bush, which reduces the cedar of Lebanon to ashes. . . . . The English may think of him as they please ; this is certain, they can show no (living) poet who is to be compared to him. . . . . But he is too worldly. Contrast *Macbeth*, and *Beppo*, where you are in a nefarious empirical world." On Eckermann's doubting " whether there is a gain for pure culture in Byron's work," Goethe conclusively replies, "There I must contradict you. The audacity and

P

grandeur of Byron must certainly tend towards culture.
We should take care not to be always looking for it in
the decidedly pure and moral. Everything that is great
promotes cultivation, as soon as we are aware of it."

This verdict of the Olympian as against the verdict of the Titan is interesting in itself, and as being
the verdict of the whole continental world of letters.
"What," exclaims Castelar, "does Spain not owe to
Byron? From his mouth come our hopes and fears.
He has baptized us with his blood. There is no one
with whose being some song of his is not woven. His
life is like a funeral torch over our graves." Mazzini
takes up the same tune for Italy. Stendhal speaks of
Byron's "Apollonic power;" and Sainte Beuve writes
to the same intent, with some judicious caveats. M.
Taine concludes his survey of the romantic movement
with the remark : "In this splendid effort, the greatest
are exhausted. One alone — Byron—attains the summit.
He is so great and so English, that from him alone
we shall learn more truths of his country and his
age than from all the rest together." Dr. Elze,
ranks the author of *Harold* and *Juan* among the
four greatest English poets, and claims for him the
intellectual parentage of Lamartine and Musset in
France, of Espronceda in Spain, of Puschkin in Russia,
with some modifications, of Heine in Germany, of
Berchet and others in Italy. So many voices of so
various countries cannot be simply set aside : unless we
wrap ourselves in an insolent insularism, we are bound at
least to ask what is the meaning of their concurrent testimony. Foreign judgments can manifestly have little
weight on matters of form, and not one of the above-
mentioned critics is sufficiently alive to the egregious

shortcomings which Byron himself recognized. That he loses almost nothing by translation is a compliment to the man, a disparagement to the artist. Scarce a page of his verse even aspires to perfection; hardly a stanza will bear the minute word-by-word dissection which only brings into clearer view the delicate touches of Keats or Tennyson; his pictures with a big brush were never meant for the microscope. Here the contrast between his theoretic worship of his idol and his own practice reaches a climax. If, as he professed to believe, " the best poet is he who best executes his work," then he is hardly a poet at all. He is habitually rapid and slovenly; an improvisatore on the spot where his fancy is kindled, writing *currente calamo*, and disdaining the " art to blot." " I can never recast anything. I am like the tiger; if I miss the first spring, I go grumbling back to my jungle." He said to Medwin, " Blank verse is the most difficult, because every line must be good." Consequently, his own blank verse is always defective—sometimes execrable. No one else—except, perhaps, Wordsworth—who could write so well, could also write so ill. This fact in Byron's case seems due not to mere carelessness, but to incapacity. Something seems to stand behind him, like the slave in the chariot, to check the current of his highest thought. The glow of his fancy fades with the suddenness of a southern sunset. His best inspirations are spoilt by the interruption of incongruous commonplace. He had none of the guardian delicacy of taste, or the thirst after completeness, which mark the consummate artist. He is more nearly a dwarf Shakespeare than a giant Pope. This defect was most mischievous where he was weakest, in his dramas and his lyrics, least so where he was strongest, in his mature satires. It is almost transmuted into an excellence in the greatest of these, which is by design and in detail a temple of incongruity.

If we turn from his manner to his matter, we cannot claim for Byron any absolute originality. His sources have been found in Rousseau, Voltaire, Chateaubriand, Beaumarchais, Lauzun, Gibbon, Bayle, St. Pierre, Alfieri, Casti, Cuvier, La Bruyere, Wieland, Swift, Sterne, Le Sage, Goethe, scraps of the classics, and the Book of Job. Absolute originality in a late age is only possible to the hermit, the lunatic, or the sensation novelist. Byron, like the rovers before Minos, was not ashamed of his piracy. He transferred the random prose of his own letters and journals to his dramas, and with the same complacency made use of the notes jotted down from other writers as he sailed on the Lake of Geneva. But he made them his own by re-casting the rough ore into bell metal. He brewed a cauldron like that of Macbeth's witches, and from it arose the images of crowned kings. If he did not bring a new idea into the world, he quadrupled the force of existing ideas and scattered them far and wide. Southern critics have maintained that he had a southern nature and was in his true element on the Lido or under an Andalusian night. Others dwell on the English pride that went along with his Italian habits and Greek sympathies. The truth is, he had the power of making himself poetically everywhere at home ; and this, along with the fact of all his writings being perfectly intelligible, is the secret of his European influence. He was a citizen of the world ; because he not only painted the environs, but reflected the passions and aspirations of every scene amid which he dwelt.

A disparaging critic has said, " Byron is nothing without his descriptions." The remark only emphasizes the fact that his genius was not dramatic. All non-dramatic art is concerned with bringing before us pictures of the world, the value of which lies half in their truth, half in the amount of human interest with which they are invested. To scientific accuracy few poets can lay claim, and Byron less than most ; but the general truth of his descriptions is acknowledged by all who have travelled in the same countries. The Greek verses of his first pilgrimage,— e.g. the night scene on the Gulf of Arta, many of the Albanian sketches, with much of the *Siege of Corinth* and the *Giaour*—have been invariably commended for their vivid realism. Attention has been especially directed to the lines in the *Corsair* beginning—

> But, lo ! from high Hymettus to the plain,

as being the veritable voice of one

> Spell-bound, within the clustering Cyclades.

The opening lines of the same canto, transplanted from the *Curse of Minerva*, are even more suggestive :—

> Slow sinks, more lovely ere his race be run,
> Along Morea's hill the setting sun,
> Not, as in northern climes, obscurely bright,
> But one unclouded blaze of living light, &c.

In the same way, the later cantos of *Harold* are steeped in Switzerland and in Italy. Byron's genius, it is true, required a stimulus ; it could not have revelled among the daisies of Chaucer, or pastured by the banks of the Doon or the Ouse, or thriven among the Lincolnshire fens. He had a sincere, if somewhat exclusive, delight in the storms and crags that seemed to respond to his nature and to his age. There is no affectation in the expression of the wish, " O that the desert were my dwelling-place !"

though we know that the writer on the shores of the
Mediterranean still craved for the gossip of the clubs.
It only shows that—

> Two desires toss about
> The poet's feverish blood;
> One drives him to the world without,
> And one to solitude.

Of Byron's two contemporary rivals, Wordsworth had
no feverish blood ; nothing drove him to the world
without ; consequently his " eyes avert their ken from
half of human fate," and his influence, though perennial,
will always be limited. He conquered England from
his hills and lakes ; but his spirit has never crossed the
Straits which he thought too narrow. The other, with
a fever in his veins, calmed it in the sea and in the cloud,
and, in some degree because of his very excellencies, has
failed as yet to mark the world at large. The poets'
poet, the cynosure of enthusiasts, he bore the banner of
the forlorn hope ; but Byron, with his feet of clay, led the
ranks. Shelley, as pure a philanthropist as St. Francis
or Howard, could forget mankind, and, like his Adonaïs,
become one with nature. Byron, who professed to hate
his fellows, was of them even more than for them, and so
appealed to them through a broader sympathy, and held
them with a firmer hand. By virtue of his passion, as
well as his power, he was enabled to represent the human
tragedy in which he played so many parts, and to which
his external universe of cloudless moons, and vales of
evergreen, and lightning-riven peaks, are but the various
background. He set the " anguish, doubt, desire," the
whole chaos of his age, to a music whose thunder-roll
seems to have inspired the opera of *Lohengrin*—a music
not designed to teach or to satisfy " the budge doctors of

the Stoic fur," but which will continue to arouse and delight the sons and daughters of men.

Madame de Staël said to Byron, at Ouchy, "It does not do to war with the world : the world is too strong for the individual." Goethe only gives a more philosophic form to this counsel when he remarks of the poet, " He put himself into a false position by his assaults on Church and State. His discontent ends in negation. . . . . If I call *bad* bad, what do I gain ? But if I call *good* bad, I do mischief." The answer is obvious : as long as men call *bad* good, there is a call for iconoclasts : half the reforms of the world have begun in negation. Such comments also point to the common error of trying to make men other than they are by lecturing them. This scion of a long line of lawless bloods—a Scandinavian Berserker, if there ever was one—the literary heir of the Eddas—was specially created to wage that war—to smite the conventionality which is the tyrant of England with the hammer of Thor, and to sear with the sarcasm of Mephistopheles the hollow hypocrisy—sham taste, sham morals, sham religion—of the society by which he was surrounded and infected, and which all but succeeded in seducing him. But for the ethereal essence,—

> The fount of fiery life
> Which served for that Titanic strife,

Byron would have been merely a more melodious Moore and a more accomplished Brummell. But the caged lion was only half tamed, and his continual growls were his redemption. His restlessness was the sign of a yet unbroken will. He fell and rose, and fell again ; but never gave up the struggle that keeps alive, if it does not save, the soul. His greatness as well as his weakness lay, in the fact that from boyhood battle was the breath of his being. To tell him not to fight, was like telling Wordsworth not to reflect, or Shelley not to sing. His instrument is a trumpet of challenge ; and he lived, as he appropriately died, in the progress of an unaccomplished campaign. His work is neither perfect architecture nor fine mosaic ; but, like that of his intellectual ancestors, the elder Elizabethans whom he perversely maligned, it is all animated by the spirit of action and of enterprise.

In good portraits his head has a lurid look, as if it had been at a higher temperature than that of other men. That high temperature was the source of his inspiration, and the secret of a spell which, during his life, commanded homage and drew forth love. Mere artists are often mannikins. Byron's brilliant though unequal genius was subordinate to the power of his personality ; he

> Had the elements
> So mix'd in him, that Nature might stand up
> And say to all the world—" This was a man."

We may learn much from him still, when we have ceased to disparage, as our fathers ceased to idolize, a name in which there is so much warning and so much example.

GILBERT AND RIVINGTON, PRINTERS, ST. JOHN'S SQUARE, E.C.

For EU product safety concerns, contact us at Calle de José Abascal, 56–1°,
28003 Madrid, Spain or eugpsr@cambridge.org.

www.ingramcontent.com/pod-product-compliance
Ingram Content Group UK Ltd.
Pitfield, Milton Keynes, MK11 3LW, UK
UKHW010336140625
459647UK00010B/643